# Romania: Rude & Vile?

By Rupert Wolfe Murray

Romania: Rude & Vile?

ISBN: 9798393433260

Copyright Rupert Wolfe Murray, 2023
Published by the author

Copyeditor: Lara Wolfe Murray
Cover art: James Hutcheson
Layout: Daoud Sarhandi-Williams

Short extracts from the following books are acknowledged:


My chapter title: *Why Romania?*
Book title: *Kitchen Confidential:*
*Adventures in the Culinary Underbelly*
by Anthony Bourdain
Ecco, Random House Group, 2000

My chapter title: *I was wrong about the Roma minority*
Book title: *I Met Lucky People:*
*The Story of the Romani Gypsies*
by Yaron Matras
Penguin, 2015

My chapter title: *Beautifully Written but Unconvincing*
Book title: *The Last Hundred Days*
by Patrick McGuinness
Bloomsbury, 2012

From my Preface:
Book title: *Further Along the Road Less Travelled*
by Dr Scott Peck
Touchstone, 1998

This book is dedicated to the people who helped make it happen:


Lara Wolfe Murray
Roxana Morea
Tim Manning
Sorina Stallard
Sönke Martin

# CONTENTS

"It is only a few months since I was there and everything
is out of date already: it belongs to history."

Graham Greene
*The Lawless Roads,* 1939


"There are two ways to edit a collection of lectures: the
easy way and the hard way. The easy way is to simply
transcribe audiotapes, correct the grammar, and print them,
even though the result might be a hodgepodge of unrelated
subjects. The hard way is to try to take these disparate
subjects and, weaving in new material, create
an imaginative, unified, and easily readable whole."

Dr Scott Peck
*Further Along the Road Less Travelled,* 1993

# INTRODUCTION

Are you wondering what kind of book this is? It isn't a guidebook, a memoir, a novel, or some kind of attempt at comedy. It's also not an up-to-the-minute report on Romania – some of it dates back to the revolution of 1989. It's a collection of stories about travelling, politics, history and people. I sent the manuscript to a Romanian friend called Roxana Morea and she described it thus: "for me, as a reader, this is a story about how much you like / love Romania and its people, the meagre and unassuming ones. And how you would like to come back here and live the rest of your life, at the end of your travels, far from the madding crowd, in some remote hamlet, completely unspoiled by the modern world's must-haves and must-dos."

This book shows some of my impressions from a country that is ancient, beautiful and mysterious – but also ugly, corrupt, poor and maddening. I lived in Romania for 17 years but never understood why I felt more at home there than I do in Scotland, my homeland.

I posted some of these stories in various places: mainly on my blog but also in the Huffington Post, and one in The Guardian. One of them, Why Romania?, is even included in a book about foreigners living in Romania. I published two articles on Romania in Time Magazine but they didn't make the grade for this book. In fact, of the 60 articles I wrote on Romania only 12 can be found here. The others just weren't good enough – my harshest critic lives within me. Two of the stories in the book have never been published before: one explains the relevance of the terms *rude* and *vile* and one is based on a talk with Ion Iliescu, the first president of Romania since the execution of the communist dictator, Nicolae Ceauşescu, on Christmas day 1989.

This book is inspired by my Romanian friends and acquaintances. The quality of their comments on my blog articles was often so interesting that it inspired me to keep writing. Sometimes their comments would complement my article with new insights, making the article itself more complete and useful. Since leaving Romania I've never managed to recreate that sense of community, that responsiveness, around my articles and that's another reason I'd like to go back and live there.

To Romanians I offer a foreigner's perspective on what is, I believe, one of the most interesting countries in Europe. I want to show my Romanian friends some of the stories I've written about their homeland and to share my opinions with them. Hopefully I can offer some fresh insights and a dash of wit. I also want to introduce outsiders to the wonders of Romania and the best way of doing this is to show the good as well as the bad. Romania is often seen negatively as, internationally, it's often lumped together with the less developed countries of south-eastern Europe. The truth is a lot of bad things do happen in Romania, as they do in every country, but lots of good things happen too, and there are many ways Romania has had a positive influence on the world. My daughter Lara, who edited the manuscript, wrote these words about the positive effect of Romanians: "Specifically Sebastian Stan's entire existence." For those who don't know the superhero genre, this handsome Romanian-American actor plays Bucky Barnes in the Marvel films.

The title I chose for this book reflects the contrast between reputation and reality, between bad perceptions and good experiences. If someone were to ask what my main impressions of the Romanian people are, I would say "they're overwhelmingly friendly and honest". If I was to discuss this book with a marketing person they would probably ask me "who's it aimed at?" I have a neat answer to this: it's aimed at Romanians who want to read old stories about their homeland. It's also aimed at people from other countries who are visiting Romania, maybe for work (Romania has been quietly accumulating a lot of investment over the last 30 years), people who have bought a guidebook and maybe a novel or history book and are looking for something else, a book with a touch of humour and madness, some light relief from reading about Romania's tragic history and politics.

Let me know if you like what you read here (or if you don't; negative feedback is also useful). Hearing from people like you is what keeps me writing.

Rupert Wolfe Murray
www.wolfemurray.com

# WHY ROMANIA?

I came across a book that helped me answer a question that had needled me for most of the 17 years I lived in Romania: why did I love to live in Romania? People asked me that question ever since I came to live in Romania, in 1990, and my answers – "the people … the warmth … the challenges …" – always felt a bit unconvincing. I was strangely unable to explain what it was that kept me there for so long. Anthony Bourdain, author of *Kitchen Confidential: Adventures in the Culinary Underbelly,* one of the funniest books I've ever read, gave me the answer even though he doesn't mention Romania once in the book.

This is his description of investing in the restaurant business in New York City: "You must be fluent in not only Spanish but the …. You must be fluent in not only Spanish but the Kabbala-like intricacies of health codes, tax law, fire department regulations, environmental protection laws, building codes, occupational safety and health regs, fair hiring practices, zoning, insurance, the vagaries and back scratching of liquor licences, the netherworld of trash removal, linen, grease disposal. And with every dime you've got tied up in your new place, suddenly the drains in your prep kitchen are backing up with raw sewage, pushing hundreds of tons of impacted crap into your dining room; your coke addled chef just called that Asian waitress who's working her way through law school a chink, which ensures your presence in court for the next six months; your bartender is giving away the bar to underage girls from Wantagh, any one of whom could crash Daddy's Buick into a busload of divinity students, putting your liquor licence in peril, to say the least; there's the ongoing struggle with rodents and cockroaches, any one of which could crawl across the Tina Brown four-top in the middle of a dessert course; the dishwasher just walked out after arguing with the busboy, and they need glasses now on table seven; immigration is at the door for a surprise inspection of your kitchen's green cards; the produce guy wants a certified check or he's taking back the delivery; you didn't order enough napkins for the weekend – and is that the New York Times reviewer waiting for your hostess to stop flirting and notice her?"

Inspired by Bourdain, I wrote a similar description about Romania: Why would anyone want to run a business in a country where government agencies send squads of inspectors to healthy businesses, like swarms of locusts, seeking out bribes, free meals, free produce and – if neither are forthcoming in the quantities expected – immediate payment of draconian fines for laws that were probably dreamt up the week before by a government that can issue scores of Emergency Orders in a late night session; laws that can go into immediate effect; with a judiciary who stood by when beefy ex-secret police thugs gained control (allegedly by illegal means) of swathes of the economy and the media – and some would say the government; where the health, educational and social services are in such a state of bankruptcy that if you end up in hospital for an operation you have to buy your own drugs and bribe the doctors, surgeons, nurses – even the cleaners – if you want to emerge in one piece; a country that has only managed to build a few hundred kilometres of motorway, at inflated prices, over twenty years, whereas the neighbouring country of Hungary (which also had no motorway in 1990) has managed to build a nationwide motorway network that Romanians can enjoy when they emigrate to a better life in Western Europe.

Within the Romanian context of legislative unpredictability, low wages, high costs, bankrupt public services and hordes of rapacious inspectors roaming the streets, you can understand why Romanians despair about their homeland and would welcome the opportunity to go west. And within their mindset of cynicism, fatalism and despair, it's logical to ask a foreigner like me "What the hell are you doing in a place like this?"

*

I first came to Romania in 1986 and it was a horrible experience. Never had I seen such sad and desperate looking people. It was only when I went to Russia, many years later, long after the fall of communism, that I saw people even more miserable looking. Nobody would look at me or speak to me and I thought I had discovered the worst country on earth. I hated it. But when I came back to Bucharest in early 1990, just after they had overthrown one of the worst communist dictators in the region, I discovered that the Romanian people are open, warm and communicative. I realised that their natural warmth had been suppressed by communism, which relentlessly instils fear, cynicism and suspicion in people. Even today there is a superficial appearance of hostility in shops and restaurants which is, I think, a hangover from communism. But if you get invited home by a Romanian you are likely to be treated like royalty. I was hooked. For almost twenty years I felt more at home there than I did in the UK, or in the other parts of Eastern Europe that I ended up living and working in.

Reading that book by Bourdain made me realise that Romania, rather like the restaurant trade, is a hostile place to do business in. But many places in the Western World have terrible bureaucracies – dealing with stubborn officials, and Byzantine rules, seems to be one of the costs of doing business anywhere. And while some people would run a mile from all this, there are people like me who thrive on it. Working in Romania is one challenge after another and nothing motivates me like a challenge – they give me purpose, energy and focus. I've worked on some big issues like child trafficking (which operates under the guise of international adoption), a Gypsy / Roma policy for the government, distributing EU grants, and I published an article in Time Magazine about a mass grave of Jews from 1941 that was only recently discovered.

From a creative point of view I think Romania is more interesting than the west and it's certainly a lot cheaper. As a writer, amateur photographer and occasional documentary filmmaker it was an ideal location as I had access to endless material and countless unique places to explore. The traditional architecture, especially in the ancient villages, looks unique and if, unlike me, you know your architectural history, traces of Russian, Ottoman and Parisian influences can be seen. Romania is unspoiled in so many ways that it's the ideal place for anthropologists, sociologists, historians, ornithologists and environmentalists – not to mention artists and writers who can find low-cost cottages in remote villages or thick forests. And don't get me started on why Romania is such a great destination for anyone into hiking or mountain biking. In conclusion all I can say is, "go there before the forces of modern capitalism destroy its unique characteristics."

# HOW THE WORDS RUDE & VILE EXPLAIN ROMANIA

I like to play with foreign languages. I love to search out funny words, to practise them in ridiculous ways and make a fool of myself. This creates an immediate bond with non-English speakers, as everyone loves to listen to a fool. It also helps me learn languages fast. This playful approach can also be used when explaining the Romanian language to foreigners. For example I might say, "The best thing you can eat in Romania is crap: crap and chips or crap soup." They look at me in disbelief, but then I tell them that the Romanian word for the fish carp is … crap. And there are lots of other words that can be made fun of; the Romanian for "I don't know" sounds like "new stew". If you hear a Romanian say, "fuck you", and thumping his chest, he's probably saying "I'll do it" (fac eu).

And this brings me to the offensive title of this article: Rude & Vile. What I like about this title is that it will, hopefully, create all sorts of wrong impressions – which I can then overturn. People will look at it and think *How dare he say that*? This is an outrage! An insult to our country! But then, if they keep reading, they'll realise that I'm using the Romanian meaning of those words, not the English.

Although this is its first publication, I wrote this article in 2018 when the government of Romania was *rude, vile* and nationalistic and I was quite happy to offend them and their supporters. Nationalism is a poisonous tool that enables people to blame everything on outsiders. At the time of writing there was a trend in Romania to blame all the ills of the nation on the Hungarian-born, American billionaire George Soros. All kinds of elaborate conspiracy theories have been built around this well-meaning Jew and even American nationalists, such as Trump and his MAGA mob, have jumped on the blame-it-on-Soros bandwagon. The convenience of conspiracy theories is that nationalist politicians, and their propagandists, can use it as a technique to absolve themselves of any responsibility. Nationalism offers a coherent narrative that blames poverty and corruption on outsiders and / or internal minorities. Part of Romania's media peddles the myth that the country's industry was sold off after the revolution and the Romanians have been reduced to the role of passive consumers within the EU – there's some truth in this but not the way the Romanian media tell it; the fact is that Romania has a large and diverse industrial base.

By now, my Romanian friends will have worked out that I've just taken two of their words and made fun of them. In Romanian, the word rude means relatives, as in aunts and uncles and cousins. And the word *vile* is the plural for villa, as in a big house and not the Mexican revolutionary leader Pancho Villa. Having explained my rather pathetic joke, this would be a good moment to end this article. But there's more – I have a theory that the words *rude* and *vile* really do help explain how Romania functions and looks.

But first, I must state for the record that I don't think Romanians are rude or vile, in the English sense of the words. If I had to choose two words that sum them up as a people I'd say friendly and honest. You can find this out for yourself by travelling around the country and being open to conversation (many of the young people are now fluent in English). I found that not only are Romanians willing to invite you home, feed and house you for no charge, but they're genuinely interested in what you think. They're warm, passionate people and I love them.

But their friendliness and warmth comes with a proviso – the first impressions are often rude and vile. People working in restaurants, shops, taxis, and the public sector, seem to have learned that treating customers like suspects in a criminal investigation is the done thing. I think this is partly because this was the style of customer service under communism when the role of the shopkeeper was to keep order while hundreds queued outside. The other thing to bear in mind when meeting Romanians is that their innate warmth is often covered by a superficial look of sadness, fed by ancient grievances, conspiracy theories and ongoing political crises.

However, the rudeness you can find in shops, restaurants and taxis is only skin deep. All you have to do is give it a few minutes and the beefy taxi driver will be giving you a detailed political analysis; the shopkeeper will be friendly; the waiter will become helpful and the public servant will help you navigate the bureaucracy. This is what happened to me time and again, since 1990, and when I hitchhiked around Romania in 2018 it was the same. Many Romanians have told me "this happens to you because you're a foreigner", but I think it happens because I'm trusting, interested in people and I try to listen. I love this contrast – a thin layer of superficial hostility covering a deep well of warmth and friendliness.

### The story of my stolen bikes

I've had two bikes stolen in my life – a Cannondale in Edinburgh and a Brompton in a Romanian village. At the police station in Edinburgh I asked the copper how I could prevent my next bike from being stolen and he said: "build a brick wall round it, with a concrete roof and no door. And they'll still get it." In the Romanian village of Humor, the local policeman actually recovered my beloved Brompton. I couldn't believe it as I had never heard of a police force anywhere in the world finding a stolen bike; I assume that most police forces don't even bother looking.

My view is that Romanians are aware of their terrible reputation abroad and are determined to show that they personally are not dishonest. I've lost count how many times I've left wallets, phones and other things in Romanian restaurants and park benches and people come running after me to give them back. It's the ideal country if you're scatty and forgetful as most people around you will look after you. And just ask anyone in the UK what they think of the Romanians they've come across; they may mention a tradesman, doctor or IT person they know and talk about them in the most glowing terms. What's clear is that when they emigrate they're driven to work extra hard and be more honest than the Pope. That's what I think of the Romanians. Now for the main course, my main point, which is: The word *rude* helps explain how Romania works.

My British relatives are a distant network of gentlefolk who meet up every ten years or so at weddings and funerals. They're charming and successful and we always say to each other "We must stay in touch", but we don't. It wouldn't cross my mind to ask them to pull strings, win contracts and get jobs – although they have always responded generously when I'm doing a charity fundraiser.

In Romania, someone in a public institution or a position of wealth will get requests for favours from relatives and they may come under social pressure to comply. This isn't to say that every public official is corrupt or that everyone indulges in these ancient practices, but it seems to be the way things are organised – a network of personal contacts is a way of getting things done in a country where the bureaucracy is dysfunctional and the laws don't make much sense. It's more subtle than just relatives helping each other out. It's about building a network of people in the right places. Underlying all this is suspicion – a tendency to not trust anyone outside a narrow circle of family and old friends. Some would say that this trait has helped the Romanians survive centuries of rule by cruel foreign empires.

This contrasts with the UK, at least my experience of it, where trust between people, and businesses, seems to be the starting point in most exchanges. In fact, it's probably one of the foundations of capitalism itself. The other big difference between Britain and Romania, the only two European countries I know well, is that the bureaucracy works in the UK – the rules and regulations are more logical and functional than in Romania. For example, if you want a passport or driving licence in the UK you just send in a form or apply online; you pay a fee and they post it back to you within a week or so. In Romania you have to go to an institution in person, stand in a queue, and fill in a complicated form and wait for ages. I may be wrong about this and it's all been improved in my absence, but I'd be surprised and most Romanians I meet complain bitterly about their bureaucracy.

Romania adopts laws without thought for their implementation, for example, they adopted the UK's entire health and safety regulations without the (essential) support structures. They have such a dog's breakfast of laws that it's a wonder how things work at all. But they do, and things function relatively well considering the hostile environment that private businesses find themselves in. Whenever a Romanian tells me his / her country has gone to hell in a handbasket, I remind them that public transport and the utilities do actually work. I learned to appreciate the value of functioning utilities when visiting Bosnia-Herzegovina during its war in the 1990s. My Romanian interlocutors will reluctantly agree and say "Ah, but the utility companies are all controlled by foreigners", which is true, and also "We get overcharged" which is probably also true. The fact is that most Romanian utilities have been privatised in the interests of efficiency and while these services are indeed more efficient in the cities, the large number of people living in the countryside remain disgracefully neglected.

You might be wondering why Romania is such a good country to invest in and the answer can be said in two words: accountants and lawyers. These modern wizards navigate the bureaucracy, make sense of the laws, and can even keep their foreign clients in a state of ignorance about any bribes that need paying. You may disapprove of this, you may call it corruption, but is it worse than British law, which allows big companies to legally avoid tax and invest their profits in offshore tax havens? Britain's big advantage is that we've had hundreds of years to embed our corruption into the establishment, and give it a sheen of respectability, whereas in Romania it's raw and obvious.

Considering the dysfunctionality of Romania's system, how do things work? The answer is corruption and *rude* – the network of contacts people use. There is corruption at every level of the system and without it nothing would work. Every family pays small bribes to teachers, officials and even priests – in order to get things done – but they're not considered bribes. Every Romanian knows that these public officials are badly paid and the bribe they're handing over is more like a tip or an undeclared service charge. It's also an insurance policy: people in hospitals know they must tip everyone down to the nurses and cleaners if they don't want to be neglected. During 2018, the government hugely increased the salaries of hospital doctors but didn't invest in the nurses, other staff or hospital infrastructure – thus making the health service even more dysfunctional.

But how does corruption work? I don't really know as I've never got involved in it, despite the fact that I lived in Romania for over 15 years. It seems to be a system that Romanians learn from childhood by observing their parents and understanding how things function. They just know when to pay a tip to the doctor or teacher and how to do it discreetly – something I never learned; the very idea of it would make me cringe in embarrassment. This is not to say that I'm purer than the driven snow. Although I never wanted to learn about corruption, and how to do it discreetly, I did once pay a bribe – to a traffic policeman who stopped me for speeding. He said, "If you want to make a payment, put it inside that piece of paper." I used to get stopped a lot for speeding but was only once asked that one time for a bribe. On the other occasions I was stopped for speeding I would either get a fine or manage to talk my way out of it by playing the hapless foreigner, hanging my head in shame and accepting his lecture on public safety.

Over the years I spent in Romania I must have sent out a signal that I want no part of this system and as a result nobody, except that traffic policeman, ever asked me for a bribe. Or maybe they didn't ask because it's an unspoken thing and I didn't know what to do. My point is that I was able to stay aloof from it and get things done correctly – thus proving that bribery isn't the only option. What did worry me were the big career-changing opportunities that came up during my time in Romania, like working for a corrupt mayor or for a dodgy international company like Cambridge Analytica, who tried to recruit me for the 2016 Romanian election. I realised that the only asset I really have is my reputation, and if I had ever gone for the quick-buck-corrupt-opportunity I might not have been trusted to work as a well paid consultant, and I certainly wouldn't have been able to fundraise for my book projects.

I can partially answer the question about how corruption works with the word rude, i.e. if you have a relative on the inside you can approach them and ask for a favour. Another key element in the system is what the Romanians call pile, pronounced *pee-lay*, which directly translates as file, as in a metal file that a prisoner would use to file through the bars and escape. What it really means in this context is useful connections, and I like the metaphor of the metal file as those tools are used to slowly wear something down, just as you can gradually apply more pressure over time to reduce your relatives' reluctance to help.

The best way to explain this is with an example from the village of Varfu Campului, which translates as top of the fields, where I lived in the early 1990s. I used to run a project in a home for abandoned kids back then and I wanted to set up a business which could make a profit for the charity. I had various ideas and spoke to the local mayor. When I told him I wanted to set up a business in his village and look for investors he got excited and said: "I can arrange everything. Just leave it to me." I was taken aback by his confidence as Romania had only just emerged from under the shadow of communism two years earlier, and doing business in the country was fiendishly complicated. Since then, the red tape has been slashed and it's much easier to set up a company (it's in the tax department where the bureaucratic monsters still reside).

But what did he know about business? He was the mayor of a village and his background was in the local collective farm. He was just a fat peasant with a tie. How would he negotiate all the licences, approvals and paperwork and why would he bother? What was in it for him? Gradually I worked out his perspective. A western mayor faced with the same question would simply have referred me to the relevant public sector authority, and I would have been shown the relevant procedures, given a link or a brochure, but this guy saw it as a personal business opportunity. He understood my question as meaning, I want you to become a full partner in my new business. All you have to do is help us register with the authorities and sort out the paperwork. That will open the floodgates to an endless flow of cash.

He also, presumably, thought there would be short term cash available which he would distribute with largesse in the county capital – thus building himself a new network of contacts (*pile*) who could be called on later when needed.

We hadn't even discussed what type of business we were thinking about; it was just an idea at that stage, for a bakery, and he didn't seem to have the capacity for discussing ideas. He thought I was offering him the opportunity of a lifetime, so he grabbed it with both hands. Needless to say the conversation ended there, but I did learn some useful lessons about working in Romania. This well-meaning mayor had offered to help navigate the bureaucracy as he knew he was more likely to succeed setting up the business, by shouting at public officials in the county capital, than we'd have been able to do by following the Byzantine rules.

Enough about *rude* – now it's time to talk about *vile*.

As I mentioned above, the word *vile* is the Romanian word for villas. A villa has a noble origin as a big house in ancient Rome and if you look it up on Google it sounds quite good: "a large and luxurious house in its own grounds". But in Romania the *vile* are a plague on the landscape for the simple reason that most of them are too big, badly designed, painted in horrible colours, surrounded by huge fuck-off-I'm-rich walls and they ruin the look of whatever community they're located in. Almost all of the old houses in Romania, especially those built prior to the Second World War, look so much better than the modern monstrosities.

If you've made a pile of cash by using your network of *rude*, the first thing you do is go and build yourself an outrageously ugly villa. This is not to say that all new houses are ugly, there are some beautiful examples of traditional house renovations, or that all rich people in Romania made their money corruptly; there are plenty of opportunities to make millions by running businesses well. One of the best things about Romania is the villages, as the people are friendly, the landscape is often beautiful, and their traditional way of life is fascinating. In fact, Romanian villages so inspired me that I think the best way to save the planet from global warming is for most of humanity to live as the traditional Romanian peasants do (or did): on smallholdings, caring for the land, keeping busy, and undermining the planet-destroying force of factory farming. It would also be a good way to create employment for all those young people who will soon be without work because of AI. Many Romanian people reading this would point out the poverty in these villages, which is terrible, but I see them as a model of life that could, if properly invested in, save our species.

The most interesting villages in Romania are the poorest ones, in counties like Caraş-Severin, located in the west of Romania, along the great River Danube, on the border with Serbia, and Vaslui which is on the north-eastern border. Rich people, tourists and ordinary Romanians don't seem to want to go to these places and, as a result, they're relatively unspoilt – at least they were when I last visited. In the old days the peasants would build houses tightly next to one another, leaving plenty of space at the back for a yard and kitchen garden, using homemade material and colours they'd mixed up locally. All the local lads would help out with the labour, most of whom learned how to build houses. I saw this happening in the village I lived in during the early 1990s, and I was deeply impressed. Ever since Romania became part of the global market they've been swamped with plastic-based paints and all the other building materials that supposedly make our lives better. Every village was also festooned with young people but today most of them have moved to low paid jobs in Western Europe. As a result the old vernacular, the old building style, is vanishing fast and being replaced with badly designed houses painted with brightly coloured chemicals from Germany.

The ugliest villages are near the big cities where the local big shots build their weekend villas. Any architectural charm that these areas once had has been replaced by a plague of *vile* – huge orange and blue monstrosities that are protected from non-existent burglars by high walls and alarm systems. And they're usually empty, as Mr Big and his brood also have a posh place in the city and they probably hate being in a village. As a result there's no extra people to use the local shop or fill up the village school. This is another nail in the coffin of the Romanian village.

It's happening in the city too. In Bucharest there are countless examples of beautiful old Belle Epoque (1871-1914) buildings that were knocked down and replaced with a modern horror. But it's not all grim – compared to Russia, where I worked for six months in Nijni Novgorod, the Romanians are good at preserving some of their ancient buildings. It's time to end this long story and make a concluding point, which I will keep short: The word *rude* is useful because it explains how Romania works, and the word *vile* offers insight into how the country looks.

# NORTH KOREA'S INFLUENCE ON ROMANIA

The main tourist attraction in Bucharest is a building that
was inspired by a visit to North Korea by Romania's communist dictator, Nicolae Ceauşescu (the surname is pronounced *chow-shess-coo*) in 1971. Today, its official name
is Parliament Palace. Under communism the name was
the House of the People, and foreign tourists now call it
Ceauşescu's Palace. If you believe the hype it's visible from
the moon, it's bigger than Cheops' Pyramid and over a million cubic metres of marble were used in its construction.
It's hard to find reliable information on how much it costs to
run but I came up with the figure of twenty million euros a
year; another source tells me that it cost about three billion
euros to build. Almost every foreign visitor I came across in
Bucharest would refer to it as Ceauşescu's Palace and this
feeds into the fevered narrative that Romania's dictator built
himself the biggest palace in the world. He actually built it
as the nation's administrative centre and today it houses Romania's parliament, a vast conference centre where (ironically) NATO likes to gather, an art gallery, and various other
things. The dictator's actual house was a relatively modest
villa in the Primavera area, now Bucharest's most exclusive
location for the rich and famous.

Many Romanians told me that Ceauşescu started out
quite well – he stood up to the Russians, objected to their
invasion of Czechoslovakia in 1968 and there was a relative
sense of freedom in the late sixties. For some years he was
a darling of the West – who thought his *independent role in
international affairs* would help in their struggle against the
Soviet Union. He wangled a State Visit to the USA, visiting
President Nixon, and was also a guest of Queen Elizabeth
with whom he went around London in a golden carriage. All
this changed after the dictator visited North Korea, and soon

enough the hapless politicians regretted arranging those high profile – such as David Steel, leader of the British Liberals, whose gift of a black labrador dog appeared in official Romanian photographs for many years afterwards.

My impression, after speaking to Romanians, was that Ceauşescu became a megalomaniac after that visit to Pyongyang. I'd been told *the whole North Korean population turned out to cheer him,* and from then on he wanted to organise Romania's population along similar lines. He evidently felt that his greatness needed to be appreciated on a grander scale. I was also told that Ceauşescu commissioned the vast House of the People, so he could stand on the balcony and look down the one-kilometre-long Boulevard of the Victory of Socialism where millions of his subjects would gather, cheer, march-by, and wave little flags in unison. But he was overthrown before the building project was finished or such crowds could be rounded up.

If you search for "Ceauşescu's visit to North Korea" on YouTube, you'll see how this practice of mass-leader-worship looked, and what could have happened in Romania had the 1989 revolution not ejected him from power. Romania's communist-run TV station sent a film crew on the visit and they put together a well-made presentation that, today, fits quite well into the anarchic mix of material on YouTube – you can see the North Koreans marching to the Bee Gees. Ceauşescu's personality cult had an impact on every family, as all children would have been expected to contribute to the vast parades that endlessly celebrated the dictator – not to mention the tens of thousands of tradesmen who were forced to work on the People's Palace building site, which operated twenty-four hours a day, seven days a week. My ex-wife was a schoolkid in communist-era Romania at the time and she had to take part in practice street parades, which were organised with military harshness. This was going on in every town and city. They were training the youth to worship the leader.

The Soviet Union had been the major influence on Romania's post-war architecture, but from the 1970s the North Korean brutalist influence can also be seen. And it wasn't just in the cities. In Romania's beautiful villages they demolished many of the rambling peasant homes and herded them into jerry-built concrete blocks – all of which were uninsulated and most lacked any functional utilities. Other countries in the Communist Bloc had similar building programmes but nowhere else can you find a North Korean-inspired monstrosity like the House of the People.

Now, having told you this backstory, I'd like to tell you how I came across a new perspective on the North Korean connection. This is a story I never published on my blog as I was saving it for this book. December 2014 was the twenty-fifth anniversary of Romania's revolution and the British Embassy in Bucharest organised a screening of *After the Revolution*, a film I had produced with a great filmmaker called Laurențiu Calciu. It showed what people were talking about on the streets just after the overthrow of communism. The embassy wanted to invite some journalists who had covered the revolution back in December 1989 and I was asked to help find them. I contacted some of the British journalists who'd been in Bucharest at the time but the only one willing to fly out for the event was Chris Walker, formerly of The Times. He joined Alison Mutler, who still lives in Bucharest, and myself, and we all gave a short talk.

Chris Walker told me he wanted to meet Ion Iliescu, the first Romanian president after Nicolae Ceaușescu was shot by firing squad on Christmas Day 1989. All these years later Ion Iliescu is still a divisive figure in Romania. Some Romanians consider him the one who brought stability to the country after a violent revolution, but the progressives tend to think he was a Russian stooge and they see the whole revolution as a stage-managed coup. Conspiracy theories thrive in Romania, and across the Eastern Bloc, and I think this is because they were fed lies by their governments for so long that conspiracy theories often seem to make more sense.

Iliescu became the interim (unelected) president after the revolution, and held onto the job for six months before general elections were held. In May 1990 he became Romania's first democratically elected president after the revolution, winning with a huge majority. Despite this, some say he stole the election. I've never seen any convincing evidence of this but what I did see during that election in 1990 was that the incumbent, in other word Iliescu, had all the resources of the state to organise a sophisticated election campaign – unlike the disorganised opposition. Iliescu had also done a good job of animating the corpse of the once omnipresent Communist Party and flipping all the thousands of branch offices, in every factory, town and school, into supporters for himself as saviour of Romania. Having pulled that tricky act off, Iliescu had no need to steal votes.

His reputation for divisiveness was consolidated in June 1990, just after he'd won the presidential election. Iliescu felt threatened by street protests and he summoned thousands of miners, armed with crowbars, to attack the street protesters and anyone who stood in their way. The government-controlled TV stations made it out that they'd come spontaneously, to *defend the revolution*. This was a moment of shame for Romania and a setback in its development. Prior to this moment there was great sympathy for the nation that had overthrown a brutal tyrant, but now the West realised that its new rulers were acting like a typical communist regime which cracks down on dissent then lies about it. Lying is one of the most pernicious features of communist regimes; in fact, the whole communist system is built on a lie – a promise of a better life where everyone is equal. Many Romanians, to this day, think the whole 1989 revolution was a lie – a secret coup d'etat and not a spontaneous series of protests (I don't agree with this analysis but that's another story).

Iliescu stayed in power until 1996 and then got re-elected from 2000 to 2004. His political party, the social democrats, or PSD in Romanian, still have the reputation of being nationalistic, opportunistic and corrupt. But how does one meet Romania's most notorious, living, former president? The British Embassy was no use at all so I resorted to contacting a journalistic fixer, one of those brilliant young networkers who are the lifeblood of foreign journalists – people who can work out how to get hold of virtually anyone. I've never been able to afford a fixer, or a translator – which is why I learned Romanian – but I've always admired them and knew a young one called Paul Lungu. He pulled a few strings, scratched some backs, made some calls and the very next day a meeting had been arranged.

So there we were: Ion Iliescu, Chris Walker, and myself, all sitting in an elegant reception room talking about the past. Chris wanted to know what had happened to so-and-so and I was trying to avoid controversial questions – like Who ordered the shootings in December 1989? – as the visit was arranged as a friendly catch-up rather than a journalistic grilling. Chris asked him about his time under communism and Iliescu said the regime had plenty of flaws but what made him most proud was that he helped spread education into the rural areas and to the poor. This, indeed, was a great achievement. But Chris didn't know about North Korea's influence on Romania and, getting a bit bored, I gave him a potted history. Then Iliescu interrupted me and said, in English:

"I was there."

"Where?" I replied.

"I was on that trip to North Korea."

Suddenly I was on full alert. Nothing of interest had been said thus far but this was new to me; here was a chance to learn something about that historic trip. It was like that moment in *Slaughterhouse Five*, by Kurt Vonnegut, who quietly said "I was there," when he heard an arrogant Air Force general justifying the Allied destruction of Dresden in the Second World War. I had no idea that Iliescu was even on the trip and I'm not sure if these memories have been written up anywhere (to be honest, I don't have the patience to check – these old communist leaders tend to write long and very boring memoirs). In 1971 Ion Iliescu was a youthful member of the Politburo, the communist-era cabinet that ruled the country. He was also in the Central Committee and was Minister for Youth. In other words he was a big shot; he'd risen to the top and was presumably one of Ceauşescu's favourites.

Iliescu didn't say anything about the actual visit to North Korea, but he seemed keen to talk about what happened on the long trip home (a flight via Moscow). This is my recollection of that conversation. On the plane to Moscow the Romanian leaders rubbed shoulders with a young African man, the son of a West African leader [like Donald Trump, Ceauşescu made friends with dictators all over the world]. Iliescu sat next to this African guy and heard all sorts of new political ideas about democracy and openness; it probably blew his mind as he'd only been exposed to communist ideas. Full of enthusiasm, Iliescu went to speak with Nicolae Ceauşescu who was sitting with his wife Elena on the plane. He said he'd heard some interesting political ideas from the young African and was keen to share them. Nicolae Ceauşescu didn't reply but his wife did. Apparently she pointed in the direction of the young African and said, "What? You've been listening to that nigger?"

End of conversation.

It was also the end of Ion Iliescu's career at the top of the Romanian Communist Party. Soon after he got back from that trip he was kicked out of his high-level functions and exiled to a minor publishing role in the provinces. He was never offered an explanation – another feature of communism is that they take snap decisions, sometimes affecting whole populations, and are under no obligation to offer explanations.

I've always been interested in that 1971 trip to North Korea as it seemed to change the fate of Romania, and here I was getting an insight from someone who was there. It was just a fragment of the story and I was unable to get another meeting with Iliescu as he started being investigated for his role in the massacres that took place during the December 1989 Revolution. But it helped me understand a few things. The fact that Iliescu even approached Ceaușescu with a personal observation suggests that the two of them had been friendly and that the dictator was perhaps open to ideas. Was this the moment when he was adopting a new political approach? One that was building on the cult-of-personality, the North Korean approach. Was this the moment when he could no longer handle any other viewpoints?

The Wikipedia history of Iliescu says that he challenged the dictator in terms of his policy and was marginalised as a result. But was it in fact this conversation on the flight that scuppered his career as a communist high-flyer? I hope someone finds out, or perhaps Mr Iliescu would like to send me his own version of events.

# MEMORIES OF A REVOLUTION

Romania's televised revolution was one of the most exciting events of 1989, that momentous year when country after country fell out of the crushing embrace of the Soviet Union. The fall of the Berlin Wall provided the main drama of that year and the revolutions in Poland, Hungary and Czechoslovakia were smooth and velvet compared to what happened at the end of the year in Romania. For years Nicolae Ceauşescu had ploughed his own furrow, and ignored the directives from Moscow – such as Romania will be an agricultural economy. He industrialised, got rid of the Red Army, tried to mediate in the Arab-Israeli conflict, paid off the national debt and was genuinely popular for the first few years of his reign.

I was just getting into journalism as the countries of Central Europe started to throw off the Soviet yoke. But I knew little about Romania (it was never in the news, which made me all the more curious) and hated it when I visited in 1986, three years before the revolution. I had just got my foot in the door at Scotland on Sunday, an Edinburgh-based Sunday paper when I was asked to cover the Romanian revolution, propelling me from the obscure foreign news section to the front page. On the 24th of December 1989, in the middle of the violent revolt against communism, I wrote: "The intense hatred Romanians have felt towards Ceauşescu is only now beginning to emerge." I predicted that the nation's "future prospects look grim," and I quoted Mircea Dinescu, a poet who was part of a group who had stormed the TV station and addressed the nation. It was one of the most extraordinary pieces of television I've ever seen. Never before, or since, have I seen someone talking in a TV studio in a scruffy woollen jumper. And I can't think of any other revolutions where a poet played such a prominent part.

Dinescu said that Romanians need to make a stand against, "dinosaurian Stalinism in whose belly we will one day find the corpses of those who had the courage to express their despair". He was referring to the fact that his country had been run along Stalinist lines, which was outmoded even in the communist bloc, and Romania was more closed and repressive than the other captive nations of Central Europe. About a thousand people were killed during Romania's revolution in December 1989, as the forces of communist repression tried to fight off the mob. There was a moment of no-government (was this anarchy?) and it wasn't clear what would happen next: would Ceaușescu and the fearsome *Securitate* (secret police) survive? Would the army, who had turned against the dictator, take over? Would Romania become a new type of communist regime, a re-formed one? The government that soon emerged was deeply flawed but recognisably democratic. Romanians complain bitterly about the low quality of their democracy but they do have relatively free elections (even though the parties tend to attract opportunists and money-grubbers) and a free press which is, like in the West, controlled by big business. Democracy doesn't come with a quality control warranty. Each nation must make it work in its own way, there's no instruction manual for How to Run a Democracy, no helpline, and you can't send it back.

I was burning with frustration in December 1989 as I was in the wrong place. I should have been sent to Romania as soon as the trouble started but when I suggested this to my foreign editor in Edinburgh he laughed and said, "We can't afford to send you anywhere!" This seemed absurd; my newspaper fancied itself as a national publication, on a par with The Sunday Times and the Observer, but they were taken aback by my suggestion that they spend some money on sending me to where the action was. I was far too broke to be able to get my own ticket to Eastern Europe and I spent a miserable Christmas in Scotland thinking "I should be in Romania! There's a revolution going on and I'm missing it!" I made a series of desperate calls to the London newspapers, but they weren't interested: they'd never heard of me and the decision-makers were on their Christmas holidays. Eventually I spoke to the travel editor of the Observer, who had published one of my travel articles. After some haggling he sent me to Romania as part of a group of journalists who had been rounded up to promote the ski slopes at Poiana Braşov. We flew to Romania in the first week of 1990, just two weeks after the revolution. In Britain they say "a week is a long time in politics", and for me those two weeks felt like an eternity.

Because of bad weather our plane got diverted to Constanţa Airport, located on the Black Sea, about two hundred miles to the east of Bucharest, Romania's capital. We spent our first evening surrounded by a squad of young soldiers with AK47 machine guns, who presumably had orders to hold us at gunpoint until someone decided what to do with us. We were the only people in the unheated airport that night and we huddled in a circle, bantering with each other and not feeling particularly worried by the teenagers with the machine guns as they looked more polite and nervous than we were, and none had the battle-hardened looks of the bad guys in movies. Eventually we were released, taken into town and put up in an old-fashioned hotel. I went for a late-night walk and noticed the streets were deserted, foggy, barely lit and had an eerie atmosphere. At that moment I realised that Romania was mysterious, so much more interesting than home, and I felt a determination to spend as much time as I could there. Even though I'd only met a handful of people thus far it was obvious that they were friendly and curious – the exact opposite of the Romanians I'd come across three years before, in 1986.

The next morning we were driven to Bucharest on a creaky old bus and, after some faffing about, were on another bus to Romania's main ski resort, Poiana Braşov, which is located about three hours north of the capital, in the Carpathian Mountains. At the ski-resort I did a day on the slopes and wrote a short article about *Post-Revolutionary Skiing* for the Observer (a piece that isn't good enough for inclusion here). In the lobby of the vast Hotel Alpin, the staff were glued to the only TV set – a small black and white job – where the trial of Ceauşescu's top four henchmen was being played out in real time. I left the press group in the ancient city of Braşov, and set out on my short-lived career as a freelance journalist – a foreign stringer, who only gets paid if his stuff gets published. It's the lowest form of journalistic pond life. I couldn't afford a hotel but I had the name of a friend-of-a-friend and this resulted in a free bed for the night. It was dark, almost no street lights, nobody about, and the thick snow on the ground added to the atmosphere. I had gone into a big hotel called the Aro Palace in order to use their phone, which were rare in those days, and call the friend-of-a-friend. The hotel was grand in scale but, like everything in Romania back then, run down and shabby.

After making the call and being told to wait, I wandered to the back of the vast, marble-floored lobby and stared into a small room with a glass door, the sort of room that would normally be used for meetings. There was a party going on and I stared in fascination at middle-aged couples dancing with more passion and concentration than I'd ever seen in my life. I was staring at them but they were so absorbed that none of them seemed to notice me. They were dancing to a Brazilian pop song that I'd been hearing everywhere in Romania and, for me, was the soundtrack for the revolution:

The Lambada. I think it was the contrast that captivated me – the erotic Brazilian beat, the swaying bodies, their obliviousness, all within a context of grim winter, fur coats and hats, worries about what was going to happen politically, suspiciousness, and a lingering fear of the once-all-powerful secret police.

Some weeks later I was living in Bucharest, and would spend hours every day wandering around town with my host and filmmaking companion, Laurențiu Calciu. Neither of us knew what was going on politically and I felt like a detective who noticed everything, took notes and was constantly trying to solve a puzzle – what am I going to write in my next update from Romania? We would go to government press conferences, hang out with the proper western journalists, listen to them dictating their stories down the phone to London and learn how the western media describe a revolution (many of them thought the army would take over and a new form of dictatorship would emerge).

Laurențiu was a thoughtful, handsome character who didn't say much. He was a maths teacher in a village under communism and he spent his free time watching old films in the city's *cinematec,* the State Film Archive, and when he got his hands on a cutting-edge VHS video camera just after the revolution he took to filmmaking like a duck to water. He went on to become a brilliant observational documentary filmmaker, but was held back by his distaste for the kitsch and compromises required in the film and TV industries. When we would hang about the streets of Bucharest in January 1990 he would film people arguing for hours on end, and I would hang around with him. We didn't take people to one side and ask questions, as a TV news crew might, he'd just get into the middle of a mob and follow their chaotic conversations – with incredible patience. Even though the city was full of international camera crews, none of them were filming ordinary people's conversations on the streets – as they were all shouting at the same time and it didn't seem to make any sense. But now, looking at that footage decades later, I realise that it was an outpouring of all those emotions and ideas that had been suppressed for so long and it's both fascinating and hilarious.

For a few weeks after the revolution crowds would gather around the University area and share their hopes, confusions and fears. Never before had I heard people talk so passionately about democracy, communism, capitalism, industry, agriculture and the future. Even though I didn't know any Romanian language at the time, the fact that so many of their words are similar to ours (like democrația, comunismul, capitalismul, industria, agricultura) kept me listening in the vain hope that I could somehow work out what they were going on about. We captured this moment of free expression on camera and, twenty years later, released it as a documentary film under the title *After the Revolution*. That rare moment of intense and anarchic discussion – when everything was debated and analysed on the street – was soon made redundant by the appearance of TV stations and newspapers, the uncensored media, where free debate was not only allowed, but was moderated by people who knew how to give it a sheen of respectability. These street debaters soon realised that their worst fears – economic collapse, starvation, war – were unfounded and they would probably keep their jobs, at least in the short term, and there was little point in endlessly arguing with each other on the streets. The excitement died down and we all moved on.

Today, Romania has established itself as a solid partner in both NATO and the EU. Despite all the corruption, con-fusion, populism, poverty, media-manipulation and emigra-tion, Romania's democracy has managed to hang on by its fingernails. It's also regarded by its Balkan neighbours as being quite good at taking action against corrupt politicians, the problem being that it's like Whack-a-Mole – another crooked official emerges as soon as one gets punished. Fast-forward to 2014, when I wrote this story: Despite all the interethnic hatred in this nation, the Romanians elected an ethnically German politician as their president. Considering that ethnic tensions had ripped apart their southern neighbour, Yugoslavia, this was impressive. "The results of Romania's presidential election" wrote Tony Barber in the Financial Times of 20th November 2014, "may turn out to be the most positive political event in Europe this year. It is encouraging for what it says about three things in central and Eastern Europe: its troublesome ethnic politics, the never-ending struggle against corruption, and the unfolding contest between the Euro-Atlantic alliance and Russia". Romania tends to get a bad rap in the international media, the country still gets used as a backdrop to horror stories of child abuse and criminality, and that's why I so appreciate the positive words Tony Barber wrote in the FT. There's endless material for people to whinge and moan about the state of the nation, but I think the Romanians deserve congratulations for getting rid of one of the most odious dictatorships in modern Europe and for consistently choosing the best of a bad bunch when faced with electoral choices. I am also grateful to them for being so welcoming to me personally and for always making me feel at home.

# BUCHAREST: FIRST IMPRESSIONS

The first thing a foreign visitor will notice upon arrival at Bucharest airport is the traffic jam when you drive into town. If she enquires about train or metro links from Otopeni Airport she'll hear some cynical, rude and perhaps amusing comments. Another thing she'll notice is the massive outdoor advertising banners all along the route into town. Our visitor may be impressed by the fact that her taxi driver speaks foreign languages – many do – but if she asks about Bucharest's infrastructure she'll soon find out there are no real plans, just electoral promises and unfinished projects which cost fortunes. If our friend has been to Cairo, she'll realise that the sprawling traffic jams in that city are similar to Bucharest's. She might also hear that Romania's politicians are unable to lay aside personal, clan, and financial interests and have failed, as a group, to understand the basic concept of the public interest.

Further conversation will reveal the Romanians' somewhat schizophrenic attitude towards their leaders. They distrust and despise them, as is common in the west, but there is an Orthodox religious practice at work in Romania, at least among old people, where the leader's word is law and they are considered untouchable, as if appointed by God. This attitude is sustained by fatalism, cynicism and complacency.

Our visitor may check into one of the city's fine five-star hotels. She may choose to spend all her time in the hotel as the climate is controlled, the staff are polite, the service is good and the atmosphere is calm – in other words, the exact opposite of what she'll find outside. One of the first things she'll notice if she steps outside is that the city's generous public spaces have been occupied – primarily by cars and kiosks – and that there's little awareness that public spaces should be reserved for citizens. If she is staying at the Hilton she might notice that the huge public space in front of the hotel is taken up by grotesque adverts and a car park. Not only does this spoil the view of the Royal Palace and the Athenaeum Concert Hall, both of which are architecturally impressive, it makes going for a walk dangerous because the pavements are so full of parked cars that she must walk on the road.

If she wanders down to Piaţa Romanâ she may be surprised to find that the pavements are occupied by small traders and that space for pedestrians is greatly reduced, resulting in chaotic crowd scenes. She may wonder why Romanians feel the need for a constant press of bodies. If she is staying at the Intercontinental Hotel she may go into the Universitate Metro (underground) Station, in which case she won't fail to notice the overpowering stink of bad cooking oil, and wonder how McDonald's have managed to occupy almost all of the public space in what should be Bucharest's show-piece underground station.

Most visitors to Bucharest are advised to pay a visit to Herăstrău Park. If our visitor goes there let's hope it's not when the park has been transformed into a marketing space or pop concert location. Several times a year the park becomes a venue for car shows, displays of noisy engineering or gardening equipment and every weekend scores of illegal traders can be seen taking advantage of the crowds. In the end, our visitor might be tempted to blame McDonald's, or the hapless kiosk owners for this abuse of public space, but this would be wrong. These commercial enterprises are doing what business does everywhere – pushing the limits. It's the responsibility of local government to define and defend their public spaces – and for citizens to hold them accountable for this.

# Postscript

This article was written in 2005, about fifteen years after Romania's revolution, and is really out of date. Bucharest is a city that changes constantly and many of the problems I describe here are no longer valid, for example there now is a train connection to the airport, and an underground / metro link is also being built, the McDonald's I describe in the main metro station has been swept away and the parking situation is much better. In addition Lara, my editor-daughter, said this article is full of generalisations, offensive comments and is, in places, just plain wrong. Another friend, Tim Manning, had some equally pertinent criticisms. Lara also points out that old people in Romania may be fatalistic, and servile towards political leaders, but young people are not and this is proven by the massive street protests they sometimes organise. So why include such an outmoded story in this book? Why not consign it to the rejected folder with all the other crappy articles I'd written? The answer is twofold: it fits neatly after my story about the revolution as it shows how Romania looked fifteen years after the adoption of democracy. It illustrates the on-the-street effects of the type of rough capitalism that was adopted here. Secondly, it expresses my own anger and frustration at a city that seemed to me, at the time, to be going in the wrong direction. I also find it quite funny – and rude (and one of my childhood nicknames, one of the less offensive ones, was *Rude*).

# GET ON YOUR BIKE & SEE ROMANIA

There are certain places in Europe that are known to be great for cycling. Amsterdam has been pro-bike for generations, in Copenhagen they say over three quarters of all journeys are made by bicycle; in Paris they developed one of the first mass-bike-hire systems, closely followed by London when Boris "the buffoon" Johnson was mayor. The car still rules supreme in this part of the world, aided and abetted by politicians who profit from all the businesses that buzz around the car, like flies around dog shit. One Romanian Prime Minister, Călin Popescu Tăriceanu, was a major importer of French cars, a role he didn't bother giving up when he became premier.

Bikes are seen as a form of transport for peasants, eccentrics and keep fit fanatics. In Romania, the standard advice is: *Don't go by bike*. The drivers are mad here, and the Romanians I've discussed this issue with believe it's a terrible country to cycle in. But they don't cycle and I've found the opposite: in my experience Romania is a wonderful country to ride in. Not only is Bucharest a joy to cross when the traffic is gridlocked, as I can saunter past immobilised machines that cost tens of thousands of euros, but there is a network of small country roads that lead to fascinating villages and a population still living off the land. In my own country, the UK, less than two percent of the population live in the countryside, and many of them are wealthy retirees. In Romania the figure is over thirty percent [or it was at the time of writing].

The other advantage of cycling in Romania is that nobody really does it, at least that was the case in 2014 when I wrote this article, but there's a growing population of serious-looking men on mountain bikes who clog up the main parks in Bucharest. I've never understood why intelligent-looking men buy expensive mountain bikes, with full suspension, for the city. I almost never see them in the mountains. I've heard of dedicated cycle roads in the Czech Republic and Switzerland, and many now think that cycling on the road isn't possible, or safe, without a separated bike lane, even though nobody had even heard of a bike lane for the first hundred years of bicycle history.

I think Romania is a great place to go on long journeys by bike. As soon as you get off the main road you discover another world – village life – where you can still see people on the streets, unlike in the UK where many of the villages seem abandoned. In each village, there seems to be another drama taking place, a different cast of characters, different scenery and scores of running dogs, many of which are friendly. Some of the villages have been modernised while others retain their ancient architectural charm. There are over three thousand villages in Romania and it would take a lifetime to explore them all. Another major asset that Romania has regarding cycling is the sleeper train network. From Bucharest you can get the overnight train to all the distant cities in the north of the country, like Cluj, Iaşi and Timişoara, and if you book into a first class sleeper wagon you can sleep on a real bed with proper cotton sheets. They also have second class sleeper wagons, with four or six bunks, but no room for a bike. I call these train wagons *Time Machines* as they are a throwback to how trains used to be around the time of the Second World War. Even though they go at a snail's pace they tend to leave Bucharest at a decently late hour and arrive on the other side of the country in the morning. If you work in Bucharest you can leave on Friday night, explore a remote corner of this fascinating country, get the sleeper back on Sunday night and be back at work on Monday morning.

One of these bike-train-weekend trips took me to the north-east of Romania. My journey took me to the remote

county of Botoșani, located in the far north east of Romania, on the border with Ukraine and the (former Soviet)
Republic of Moldova. Botoșani is at the end of the line,
stuck in a corner of Romania. You don't go there unless it's
your final destination, since there's nowhere further to go;
it's a dead end. Also, Botoșani is considered to be one of the
poorest counties of Romania and therefore undesirable from
the touristic point of view – but ideal for people like me
who like to visit places that aren't overrun with tourists or
spoiled by the kitsch new constructions of Romania's newly
rich.

Getting onto the sleeper train with a bike is always a bit
of a drama and the dialogue, in Romanian, with the beefy
guard usually goes like this:

"What's that you've got there?"

"It's a bike."

"You can't bring that on the train."

"But they told me I could when I bought the ticket."

"Those bloody idiots in the ticket office!"

Then I stand around looking lost, confused, and foreign.
The guard rolls his eyes and complains to whoever is listening. I try to stand in the corridor, blocking it, as this puts
them under pressure to deal with me and clear the walkway.
Meanwhile I know full well there's nothing he can do at
eleven at night as the ticket office is closed, and he's seen
my sleeper ticket which is the most expensive type of ticket
you can get, so is he going to refuse me entry? The trick is
to show humility, admit you're in the wrong, recognise their
authority, apologise. But I don't leave, as many Romanians I know would, and, with every second that passes, I let
the pressure build up in his head. It's now his problem and
invariably he just shrugs, mutters and lets me on board. I
have a Moulton Touring bike which splits in half and goes
into two black bags so they look more like large pieces of
luggage rather than a bike. I've always managed to get it

onto trains, planes and automobiles without having to resort to bribery or corruption.

After a great sleep on real cotton sheets the grumpy fat butler (each sleeper wagon has one) as in the pre-war days of good train service, woke me and mumbled "Leorda" – the tiny station I was heading to. It seemed like the whole population of Leorda, including half a dozen mutts, showed up for the train's arrival and there was pandemonium for a few minutes. Presumably it was the big event of the day. The villagers had come to meet those getting off the train, collect sacks of stuff and greet their visitors. There was a hubbub of noise as if a garden party was taking place. The crowd of villagers gradually dispersed. The train hissed, heaved, groaned and shuddered out of the village. The Station Master, in his communist-era peaked hat, wandered back into his cubbyhole, presumably to continue his sleep. Like the final curtain at the theatre, a heavy silence descended and I looked round at the only other living being in the station – a stray white dog. Silence is quite normal in the countryside but it's more pronounced when it follows the boom and hiss of an old train.

I reached the main road and headed for Dorohoi, the second-biggest town in the county; a town that was once considered the Jewish capital of Moldova. Once there, I went to the market for some fruit and cheese and was transported back in time; a time when people would banter across the marketplace, shout jokes at each other, and be more inquisitive and open than they are nowadays. The Moldavian peasants are witty, relaxed and prone to philosophising but they are becoming a rare species as market forces, and supermarkets, are making them irrelevant. Most have emigrated.

I then cycled to the small town (or is it a big village?) of Săveni, where I was planning to find a guest house and spend the night. Getting there took most of the day. I had thought that Botoşani was a flat county and that cycling across it would be easy. I was wrong on both counts. It's not flat but it's not hilly either. Botoșani has a landscape that I haven't seen anywhere else – rolling plains. The only way to describe it is to compare the landscape with the sea. If you can visualise the shape of a wave, long, regular but with no peaks, then you should be able to imagine the land of Botoșani, which looks like endless waves: ridge, followed by depression, followed by another ridge.

Although the land looked rather lush and green there didn't seem to be anyone around; there were very few cars to bother me and it all seemed rather idyllic. Every village, however poor, had at least one shop but they all seem to contain the same mass-produced products, supplied by the same distributors. But I was in no mood to contemplate the evils of globalism and supermarkets, all I wanted was something sticky, sweet and unhealthy that would give me energy. Each village shop has something that you don't find in the city – people who are keen to come out and chat. All were interested in my bike, route, sanity, and they were incredibly friendly. In one shop, in a village by a big lake, I saw that the shoppers would go into a garage-type building behind the shop. When I asked about it I was led inside and shown a stack of wooden boxes containing live fish. The shopkeeper said they'd been taken out of the lake that morning and can live without water for more than a day.

At Săveni, the town I was intending to sleep in, I couldn't believe that there was no guest house at all. This is supposedly the third-biggest town in the county yet there was nowhere for visitors to stay. I started feeling sorry for myself and wishing I'd brought my camping gear. Then I remembered a Romanian friend who'd moved to Dubai and whose parents came from this area. After a few phone calls I got an address and was off to a nearby village where I met a charming old couple and was treated like a king. Their house was scruffy and cosy, their garden large and rambling, and they plied me with their own plum brandy, lime-leaf tea and filled me up with delicious sour soup, homemade bread, pickled salad, stuffed cabbage leaves and *mamaliga,* which is a coarse form of polenta.

The next day was an epic ride up more of those incredible land waves and, before long, I was at the border with the Republic of Moldova. A huge lake marks the border as far as the eye can see and I wondered why there was nobody around. Where were the tourists in this pristine landscape with a vast and beautiful lake? Not that I was complaining, far from it, I was enjoying the fact that the road was virtually empty. Maybe one car appeared every ten minutes. Hours later I came across a young boy with a cartful of watermelons and decided it was a good moment to stop for lunch. He said his parents had moved to the watermelon field for the summer and were living in a hut down by the lake. His job was to sit by the side of the road and sell the fruit to passing motorists. He seemed quite happy with his lot. I gave him my penknife and left with a belly that was full to bursting.

I went through the small town of Ştefăneşti and then a big village where a riot seemed to be taking place. I stopped for a gawp and found it was just a bunch of drunken peasants shouting at each other across the road. I don't know why but this sort of unacceptable behaviour makes me laugh and feel relaxed. After endless fields and forests, I approached two big institutions I recognised from my aid-agency days: a prison and a lunatic asylum. I realised that I'd reached Botoşani city. I remembered a story from the 1990s – someone escaped over the high walls of the lunatic asylum and shouted, "I'm free!" But he had only managed to escape into the prison! By now it was raining cats and dogs but fortunately I had good waterproofs and managed to stay dry. By the time I got into the city centre I headed for a restaurant and stuffed myself with cooked food, which always tastes better when you've been out in the wilds. When the restaurant was closing and people were wandering home, I made my way over to the railway station and boarded the sleeper train back to Bucharest.

# HOW TO APPRECIATE POOR PLACES

I'm writing this article on the train to Tulcea, the stop-off point for Romania's Danube Delta – a vast nature reserve where the Danube River spills into the Black Sea. I'm going to the coastal village of Sfântu Gheorghe to enjoy the vast, unspoilt, and virtually empty beaches and go into the wetlands to look at birds. Most tourists who come to the Danube Delta probably don't know that it is one of the poorest areas of Romania. Wikipedia says, "The acute isolation and the harsh conditions of living, based mainly on subsistence, made the Danube Delta a place of emigration."

Some of the most interesting places I've seen are poor. Wherever you go in the world people are friendlier when they have less, and they're also more likely to be connected to their indigenous culture. I also think that a lack of visitors tends to make people more friendly, as we often get bored of each other and crave new company, new conversations. Romania is, in my view, the most welcoming place in Europe. When I went to Asia in the 1980s, Tibet and India were the friendliest but also the poorest.

But how do you visit a poor place without being exploitative? How do you compensate a person, or family, that's been friendly and maybe even offered a bed for the night? Are they doing it for money or because of the ancient tradition of hospitality which takes in strangers without expectation of reward? In my experience, friendly villagers appreciated my visit, if only for the conversation. The officials at Romania's Ministry of Tourism don't like backpacker-type travellers like me as we don't spend as much money, per head, as the mass-tourists who get flown in by the thousand and packed into high-rise hotels on the coast. But does mass-tourism really contribute that much to the economy? Doesn't all that cash being swilled around on the coastal resorts end up in foreign bank accounts of the owners? I don't have any answers to these questions, but I do think it's good to be friendly to villagers, and accept their hospitality. Apart from anything else, it's a good way to discover an interesting local community.

My approach to travelling through villages is like this: I accept that I'll never be one of them so I avoid being over-familiar; I am open, friendly, polite and I try to listen more than speak. In this way I can quickly work out who's worth dealing with and who must be avoided – drunks, scammers, who are usually over-familiar too soon, and conspiracy theorists. A key factor is realising that my visit will be appreciated if I follow my golden rules: listen, observe, don't judge and be respectful. One of the many problems of living in a poor place is that outsiders often assume it's ugly, dangerous, unhygienic and best avoided. Therefore, by simply turning up and being open, you can challenge these prejudices and show those decent local people that not all of us view them in that negative way.

The train I am on just passed the station of Fetești. It looks like a fly-blown dive from the window. The station is crumbling, alcoholic-looking people wander about aimlessly and stray dogs sleep in the shade. And yet, if I took the time to get to know the locals, I'm sure I would come across some friendly and interesting people. I'm in a constant struggle with myself to not accept the instant judgments I come up with whenever I see something, or someone, and if I make a generalisation in front of my son Luca he will quote my own words back at me: "Generalisations are always wrong!" My awareness that I can be instantly prejudiced is really helpful as I can quickly resolve the problem and start looking for the good in every situation.

The other thing you can do is try and pay people for things. When staying in a hotel or eating in a restaurant the chances of your payment reaching a local family are almost zero. The money goes to the business owner and, possibly, the local government, while your disgruntled waiter will be paid a pittance. But if you stay with a local family not only would you make them proud that you chose them to stay with, but any money you leave behind will be really appreciated both as a gesture and as a contribution towards their running costs. If you leave them even half of what you would normally pay for a night in a hotel, it would have an impact on that month's household budget.

Problem is, how do you stay with people in villages? The idea of staying with these people can seem frightening. Romanians have told me things like: "Nobody stays with the peasants! It's unthinkable! They're uncivilised! All they want is your money!" But you would be amazed how even the poorest Romanian household can make a guest feel genuinely welcome, and if you trust them they will actually protect you and your stuff – the idea of their guest being robbed would be mortifying to the traditional villager. One of the most memorable nights I spent in the Nepalese Himalayas was in a mud hut with a grass roof and just enough space for me and the family to sleep on the earth floor. It was perfect, and the earth floor had been rubbed and cleaned so much it seemed to glow and shine. It can be an honour to host a foreign guest and that's why it's so important to treat them with the utmost respect.

In 2015 Eion Gibbs walked across Europe, from the Netherlands to Istanbul, in the footsteps of the English writer Patrick Leigh Fermor, author of the classic 1933 travel book *Between the Woods and the Water*. I asked Eion how he got accommodation in the Romanian villages he would pass through, and this is what he said: "I would go to the village bar and ask where the local hotel was, even though I knew perfectly well that there was none. The locals would talk among themselves and eventually somebody would lead me off to his place and I'd be given a comfortable bed and a good meal." Sometimes it can be hard to pay for this kind of hospitality. Often they are so glad to have you to stay that the idea of paying for it can be offensive and you can't then say: "You need the money because you're poor". What I used to do in these situations was hide money under my pillow or somewhere in the room I'd slept in.

A final observation about poor places is that they can be really interesting. I'm finishing this article in the town of Medgidia, where I must wait 40 minutes for the connecting train. The station looks run-down and depressing. I wander out, past the grim-looking taxi drivers, to see what I can find. A few hundred yards down the road I find peace and quiet by the Danube Canal – a vast communist-era project where Romanian intellectuals were worked to death. I'm surrounded by curious concrete structures, all abandoned, and plenty of insects going about their business. I open my ears and hear a chorus of frogs, a dog barking, a distant horn blast (factory, ship or train?), a cockerel and a crowd of small birds engaged in a furious debate. It feels rather exotic.

I'm still on the train to Tulcea and, like most Romanian trains, it's taking forever. Their railway network was built in the nineteenth century, upgraded by the communists and neglected by the current regime of car-friendly capitalists. But this is good for me as I've got plenty of time to finish this article. The carriage is packed with sullen-looking people who, I'm sure, could be easily befriended if I made the effort, but what I like about them is that they're not giving me any dirty looks or making snide comments about the dodgy-looking foreigner writing on his fancy laptop. I'm thinking about sounds, and how at the last stop I was able to hear all sorts of interesting sounds because I consciously told myself to listen. It was almost like I was turning on my ears. But now I don't want to hear any background noises, I don't want to be disturbed by the rumbling of the train, the constant clicking sound of metal wheels on metal tracks, and so I consciously switch off my ears. This is a skill I picked up when living in the Romanian village of Vârfu Câmpului, which translates as Top of the Fields. I lived with a family that was ruled by an old lady known as Mama Puiu. She would feed us epic amounts of delicious, home-grown food but the problem was that she never stopped talking. It was there where I learned to stop listening and realised that I wasn't causing offence, as all I had to do was glance in her direction now and then and occasionally grunt to suggest I was actually listening. She didn't want a conversation, she wanted an audience. What I'm getting at is that you can try this approach if you ever want to explore a Romanian village; find an interesting place, listen out for the sounds of nature, birds, animals, wind, people working, cars going by. And you can use the switching-off the ears trick to good effect too if you realise that many people don't really want to converse, they just want an audience and if you nod politely and make appropriate sounds they may be satisfied with the conversation. What this means is that you can show up in a Romanian village with no understanding of the Romanian language, and spend a happy evening with locals. In this way you can transform the poorest and most desperate-looking dive into a fascinating experience.

# CYCLING THE CARPATHIANS

When I first heard about the Transfăgărășan road it was described with a sense of awe as the highest road in Europe, an engineering wonder by Ceaușescu who ordered it built as part of his military strategy. Northern Romania is divided from the south by the mighty Carpathian Mountains, which rise to the impressive height of 2,544 metres, but there's few crossing points. Like many dictators, Ceaușescu was paranoid and in order to prevent an imaginary-invading-army from cutting off half the country he commissioned this road across the Carpathians. It started out as a military road and is now a tourist attraction. But is it really the highest road in Europe? I have learned to be sceptical about nationalistic claims to have the biggest, highest, longest things in the world. A quick look on the internet shows that it probably isn't the highest road in Europe; but neither is the Col de la Bonette, the French claim which is challenged by the Brits from the Hidden Europe magazine who say: "There are tarmac roads in the Alps which are higher, and if you are prepared to take gravel roads into account, then many are much higher." But, at an altitude that reaches two thousand metres, the Transfăgărășan Mountain Road is no slouch.

The Făgăraș, pronounced *fag-a-rash*, mountains are the highest part of the Carpathian mountain range. The Făgăraș stretch between the ancient Romanian cities of Brașov and Sibiu and when looked at from the northern side it looks like an impenetrable wall, like a backdrop in Lord of the Rings. You can understand why the Austro-Hungarians treated it as their natural frontier with the Ottomans. For centuries it marked the border between those two great empires.

I certainly didn't feel impressive as I looked up at this endless wall of rock and thought: *What made me think I could get over that on a bike?* Just getting to the bottom of the climb was bad enough. Already I felt burned-out after cycling just seventeen kilometres on the approach road, which is on flat ground. In order to put off the inevitable climb I stopped at a roadside cafe, ate a greasy breakfast, made calls, and procrastinated. I seriously considered giving up but then called a friend, Horia Maruşca, who makes a living by doing mountain bike tours, and he made it sound easy. He would usually do it in three hours but, he said, "with all your camping gear it could take you five hours". This was my challenge: of course I could do it in under five hours! Before dragging myself out of the cosy café I called another old friend, Laurenţiu Calciu, and talked it over with him. Under communism he would often go hiking in the mountains but, like so many people, gave it up in middle age. But he was sympathetic about my procrastination, a subject in which he is an expert, and quoted Brâncuşi, the Romanian-born sculptor: "Doing things isn't hard, it's getting into the mood to do things that is hard."

After what seemed like an age, I set off with determination and energy. My breakfast sloth had been dispelled. The next ten kilometres were flat and effortless, and then the road climbed steadily over a distance of twenty-four kilometres, to a height of two thousand metres. The gentle climb lulled me into a false sense of confidence and I charged up the lower reaches like a champion cyclist, cruising past the tourists who crowded round the guest houses in the foothills, the odd campsite by the river and happy looking hikers. I must have climbed for about two hours, through endless forest, continual bends as the road switched back and forth up the mountain, all the time sheltered from the sun by the high trees. It was idyllic. Easy. Exhilarating. Almost there!

I only stopped once in the lower forested section of the climb, to drink at a roadside fountain and get energy from a Lion bar. These roadside fountains seem to attract people like flies to a honeypot and I was surprised to see so many cars from the Romanian region of Moldova, which is about a day's drive away. In Romania every car number plate has a two letter acronym for each of the forty-one counties and, after many years in the country, I had learned to identify them. It wasn't hard to understand why there were so many cars from Moldova, the eastern part of Romania, as this is one of the most dramatic tourist spots in the land. Most of the tourists I saw were Romanian but I know lots of foreigners come here too, the most famous one being Jeremy Clarkson who came to the Transfăgărășan road with three supercars and a helicopter.

Cars from almost every county in Romania passed me on this road, including a three-vehicle convoy that was driving a lot faster than anyone else. The vehicles at the front and rear of this unusual convoy were keeping as close as they could to the bigger vehicle in the middle, obscuring the view of a 4x4-shaped vehicle that had all its bodywork wrapped in black plastic. The plastic wrapping also covered the side and back windows but, presumably, not the windscreen or the driver wouldn't have been able to see. I was instantly fascinated. What was this? I had managed to get a good look at the black-wrapped Mystery Machine and the best clue I picked up was the word PROBE written in capital letters on the number plate. Probe means test in Romanian language and it didn't take a brain surgeon to work out that this was some experiment by the Dacia car company, located on the other side of the mountains, testing out their new 4x4. [2023 Postscript: that car, the Dacia Duster, the cheapest 4x4 on the market, has gone on to conquer Europe].

By now I assumed I'd broken the back of the climb, as I had done about two hours since my lazy breakfast stop and had been going pretty quickly. Surely the end was nigh? I'd emerge from the forest, cruise over the mountain tops in a blaze of glory and there might even be a cheering crowd! But when I eventually emerged from the forest I realised that the high trees had been hiding the true extent of the climb, the real horror, and I was faced with a massive wall of rock ahead, almost as high as it had seemed from the bottom. I was starting to feel like Frodo in the Lord of the Rings, making his way through the forbidding and impossible land of Mordor. I knew there was a tunnel at the top, at the height of two thousand metres, but where the hell was it? Surely it would appear any moment now, saving me having to climb up this monster, but I had a horrible sinking feeling that the real climb had only just begun. How I regretted my general lack of fitness and my disdain for training. Then I saw a distant line of roads weaving their way up into the ridge. At this point I lost all my energy, lay down by the side of the road and, even more seriously this time, considered giving up. These false summits are killers. You ration your energy to arrive at the top with style, with some reserve energy so you can enjoy the view. But the Bastard Mountain denies you this and seems to project the thought: *Aha, I've tricked you! You believed in your own arrogance. You burned up your energy too early. Serves you right! Now you can freeze in that ditch.* But the idea of going back was too humiliating, and it was too cold to stay where I was, so there was only one option: stagger on. An inbuilt autopilot took over the actual cycling at this stage, shutting down most thought processes and just shuffling me along the road like someone with a debilitating illness. I was sometimes riding, sometimes walking, just putting one foot in front of the other.

The thing that really drove me up the last section was actually the German cyclists I had cruised past earlier, feeling very pleased with myself as I left them in my wake. Now that I was shambling along like a drunk I wasn't feeling so proud, but I was wondering: Where are the Germans? They seemed so well-equipped and fit that surely they would power past in a matter of minutes, sneering at me with Teutonic superiority. But no, they too were struggling with the ride, and to my surprise they didn't overtake me. The realisation that there were others who were as weak, pathetic and unprepared as me gave a desperate form of energy and I managed to stay ahead of them all the way to the top.

All day there had been ominous black clouds hovering over the crags and the occasional grumble of thunder could be heard. But the Făgăraş range is so vast in scale that the storm seemed to wander off and expend itself in other places, leaving me in peace. Or so I thought. Just two kilometres from the top, when I had victory in sight, when my pain and exhaustion were numbed, the heavens opened and a violent downpour of hail started. I was wearing supposedly bomb-proof waterproofs, oilskins, but such was the wildness of the storm that within minutes I was soaked to the skin. But I had reached the top, and the best part of this story is that there was a guest house and restaurant right there, perched above a small lake called Bâlea Lac, beckoning me in like an evil stepmother in a fairy tale. I walked in dripping, feeling as if I'd been in a shower with all my clothes on. A guy at the door said, "I've never seen such a violent storm in all my life" and inside they gave me funny looks as I peeled off wet clothes and hung them up to dry. Although I had arrived in the restaurant on my last legs, a good meal of trout and mamaliga (pronounced *mama-leager* and known elsewhere in Europe as polenta) with plenty of unhealthy fizzy drinks soon restored me. Within an hour all that pain and despair on the way up had been forgotten and I was eager for more. The rain had stopped and my clothes were drying rapidly. I was ready to move on.

My initial plan was to spend the night at this guest house but it's a bleak and cold location and I was missing the warmth of the Romanian lowlands. Romania was in full summer mode and the temperatures had been getting up to forty degrees Celsius on the plain. I sent a message to my biking friend to report on my lame progress, about four and half hours from bottom to top, and then cycled through the eight hundred metre tunnel that took me from northern to southern Romania. If climbing a two thousand metre mountain pass is hell, and it is if you're an out-of-shape slob like me, going down is like being in heaven. But the first thing you must do is put on warm clothes under the waterproofs. There was plenty of snow lying around, and it was June! As you build up speed on the way down you need to protect yourself from the wind-chill-factor, one of the few things I remember from school: the wind makes low temperatures much colder. What a joy it was to reach high speeds and overtake the vans that seemed to be crawling along, to lean into the corners as a motorbike rider would, to feel the wind in my hair. And I couldn't help thinking about the contrast between my snail-like progress coming up and this exhilarating speed going down.

But the joyride was soon over and the road entered another endless forest. Unlike on the northern side, there are no villages for miles on this side. Maybe this whole vast area has always been uninhabited? On and on I rode, still fuelled by the delicious lunch. But as the day stretched into evening I started wondering where I could stay. I had camping gear in my panniers, which had added considerably to the bike's weight, but everyone had said there were too many bears around to risk sleeping out. After God knows how many hours, my energy started dissipating and soon enough I was struggling up the smallest rise in this endless road. But there was no sign of human habitation and I had to go on, eventually reaching the huge hydroelectric dam at Lake Vidraru. From there it was a long downhill ride into Arefu, the village made famous by its association with Vlad

Țepeș, the fifteenth century ruler of this land and inspiration for Bram Stoker's Count Dracula. You can climb a steep hill and look at the ruins of Vlad Țepeș' small fortress, which perches on a clifftop.

It was dark by the time I made it into the village and it took several hours of knocking on doors before I was able to find a guest house that would let me stay. Romania is curious in this way, sometimes people offer you free accommodation and endless amounts of food but it never seems to be on offer when you really need it. The next morning I decided to take a day off and look at the traditional cottages and beautiful woods which stretched out in every direction. I was surprised not to see any tourists coming to see Vlad Țepeș' real castle, but remembered that there are two other castles in Romania that are associated with Vlad Țepeș and the Dracula legend. Both of them are called Dracula's Castle even though historians agree that the real Vlad Țepeș never had a base at either location. The most popular of these tourist castles, in the village of Bran, dates back to the Middle Ages but the other one, located in the far north, was built in concrete by the communists and is used as a kitsch hotel and restaurant to this day.

# TRAVELLING THROUGH KITSCH

In Romania, as in every country, there are stereotypes about where you should visit and which places you must avoid. If I tell people I'm from Scotland many would say they'd love to visit Edinburgh but it's rare you hear people saying they want to see Glasgow, which is an equally great city to visit. Visitors to England will usually want to visit cities like Oxford, York or Bath, and might have misconceptions about the industrial cities like Manchester and Newcastle. The former are known for their beauty, their roles in history, or for being retreats for the upper classes. Meanwhile, the cities that rose through industrialisation have never quite shed the reputation of being poor, dangerous and ugly. Naturally, it's all a misconception. These once-industrial cities have thriving communities, vibrant streets, phenomenal cuisine from around the world, and there's no shortage of beautiful old buildings too.

In Romania they say you should visit Braşov and the fancy cities of Transylvania, but avoid Moldova and the eastern part of Romania as it's poor and therefore of no interest to anyone. I was able to test this generalisation by driving a car from Braşov, in Transylvania, to Botoşani which is in the Romanian region of Moldova – not to be confused with the formerly-Soviet-now-independent Republic of Moldova. I was on a commission for a German TV station that wanted me to find Romanians who had lost kids to the evil business of international adoption, which is a way that rich westerners can buy children – but that's another story. This job had taken me from Bucharest to Braşov and now I needed to drive on to Moldova.

Although the centre of Braşov is nicely preserved and retains much of its Saxon charm, most of the town is just endless concrete blocks – but the approach roads are crowded with advertising banners, building sites and vast retail sheds. The Brits have a saying about hypocrisy – the pot calling the kettle black – and the Romanians have a similar one: the broken bit of pottery laughs at the smashed pot. What I'm getting at is that Romanians criticise their gypsy / Roma minority for having bad taste and yet they allow some of their most beautiful old cities to be surrounded by vast advertising banners and endless retail sheds. The road from Brașov to Moldova takes you through hills, mountains and forests but the view is ruined by all the new villas that have popped up in unspoilt rural locations. These grotesque constructions are owned by local businessmen who feel the need to flaunt their wealth by showing off garish colours, stainless-steel railings, gold-tinted windows, blue roofs, and irregular angles. Lara, my daughter-editor, told me about McMansions in the USA and I see it's a problem over there too. Writing in the Spruce website, Kristin Hohenadel describes McMansions as: "A symbol of American excess, these homes reinforce the unsustainable notion that bigger is always better ... developers began bulldozing perfectly lovely human-scale houses, which often sat gracefully on generous plots of land, and replacing them with pretentious, bloated monstrosities .... Neo-eclectic in style, connoting a mishmash of sometimes unrelated architectural styles lacking in coherence and integrity – the result of the absence of an architectural style."

Traditionally, Romania had original and subtle village architecture. But maybe architecture is the wrong word as there's no way nineteenth century peasants, however wealthy they were, would have commissioned house designs from city-based architects. Not only were there not many architects around in those days but the architects themselves would have looked down their noses at such a commission. But, even today, you can see very distinctive styles of traditional houses in Romania and there must have been some collective awareness about how to build and how to apply certain styles – just as today anyone building a house in Romania is under some unspoken obligation to make it as ugly as possible. There are two main styles of traditional village house – Moldovan and Transylvanian – and I prefer the Moldovan style as they're more open, warm and welcoming. The typical Transylvanian house is, I believe, inspired by the Hungarian and German tendency to build the outer wall right on the street, which is efficient in that you don't waste space with a dinky little front garden. The facade of these buildings can be stunning, even today, centuries later: painted in locally produced pigments with all sorts of architectural, or vernacular, devices like coats of arms, brightly coloured ceramic tiles, elaborate tin guttering and proud metal cockerels standing on the rooftops as weathervanes. Next to the house-front will be a huge gate and the house, and yard, will stretch back for quite a distance, eventually reaching a huge barn. The overall look and feel of these buildings are impressive and the use of space is highly efficient as the whole thing might stretch back for hundreds of metres, almost always including a kitchen garden, and so there's space for others to build more homes on similar long, thin, plots with their narrow fronts, along the village roads. What I don't like about them is that you can't see any of that good stuff behind the high gate.

The typical Moldovan village house is, by contrast, like a fat, jovial, Turkish pasha sprawling on a divan in an open air coffee house where everyone can see him – less efficient perhaps, but so much more welcoming than those buttoned-up Transylvanians hiding behind their high gates. I have no idea where this Moldovan style comes from and I wouldn't be surprised if it was Ottoman, or Russian, but it's much less regular than the smart, uniformly laid-out Transylvanian plots. The Moldovan peasant would get hold of a piece of land and plonk his house somewhere in the middle of it. He'd plant flowers, vegetables, vines and fruit trees in every available scrap of earth, creating an overall impression of lushness. While the Transylvanian would use brick the Moldovan would probably use chirpici – pronounced *keer-peach* – a combination of mud-and-straw bricks and adobe, which is the use of mud as plaster for external walls. Such materials may sound yukky to modern ears – Building with mud! How uncivilised! – but these ancient techniques are gaining in popularity as not only are they more environmentally friendly than concrete, but they can look great too. Having assembled his pile of keer-peach, and rounded up the neighbours to help with the labour, the sturdy Moldovan peasant would then build several small, single storied buildings alongside the main house, each with overhanging tin roofs which channel rain about half a metre from the building. They don't use gutters and I've seen how efficiently these houses handle heavy rain. These extra buildings would be used for guests, animals, storage and the most important one, at least in the warm seasons, would be the outside kitchen – where the womenfolk would prepare delicious meals, based on maize and borscht, to be eaten outside, under the vines which would be growing on trellises all over these outside areas. Anyone walking by can see right into these yards and, when I lived in a Moldovan village in the early 1990s, they would shout a greeting, invite us in and ply us with smoked pork fat and an evil-smelling, clear alcohol made from fermented sugar beet.

I drove over the Carpathians and got to the Moldovan city of Bacău, pronounced *back cow*, whose architectural merit I've never discovered, and then Roman which looks like another historic Romanian town that's had its heart ripped out and replaced with concrete. The local council have attempted to improve their image by painting the blocks facing the main road, a tactic that was first done in Bacău, but their choice of reds and yellows is all wrong.

Not only are these the colours of McDonald's but it makes me think of a drunk who has clumsily applied too much lipstick and make-up. I was starting to feel depressed. What have they done to this beautiful country and their unique village buildings?

By now I was deep into the Moldovan part of Romania, in the county of Iași, pronounced *yash*, and I left the main road and drove into a village that was surrounded by forest. As in most Romanian villages that aren't located on main roads, the road was made of gravel and was full of potholes. The problem with gravel roads is that, in the dry season, you whip up great clouds of dust but the good news was that I was passing into the other Romania – the rural heart-land. When I finally reached the village I had been looking for I immediately saw that it was poor but beautiful, with original and interesting houses, each with its own garden and hand-made wooden fences. The streets were full of children, old men and livestock wandering home after a day's grazing on the common. Above it all towered ancient walnut trees. It was like stepping into a fairy tale. When I eventually tracked down the family I was looking for I saw they had their own woodpile and food supplies, hens and stores of dried maize, but it was also clear that their lives were very hard and, at least for the man of the house, the main stimulant was alcohol.

I was following up on a clue: in this village there was a woman who'd had her child taken away by social servic-es in the 1990s, kept in hospital after birth, for spurious reasons, and then sold to an American adoption agency. About 30,000 children were sold in this manner during the 1990s. Because the mother was poor and located in a village that was several hours from the county capital, it was very costly for her to reach the authorities and when she did they claimed to know nothing of her lost baby. The child traffickers would target poor women in remote villages as they knew they would struggle to reach the county capital and, even when they did, would have no clue about how to complain effectively. I subsequently wrote a formal letter to the County Child Protection Agency, and eventually found out that the baby had been sold to an American family. I came back with a cameraman and the case was presented on German TV, as part of an investigation into child trafficking.

As I drove north to the remote Moldovan city of Boto-șani, I realised that one has to find these remote locations if you want beauty and tranquillity in Romania. It seems that the further the village is from the asphalt, the more unspoilt and attractive it is. An important factor for Romania's nou-veau-riche, the ones who erect big houses in villages, is to build on the main road. Houses off the main road are worth a lot less. The result is what they call ribbon development, villages spread out over miles and miles of main road. Al-though this suits people who want to show their new-found wealth to the neighbours it also means that these villages have no centre, no heart, many have emigrated and the re-maining population is scattered along a long road. Needless to say most of these villages have no utilities.

There are some attractive cities in Moldova, such as Iași, the ancient capital city of the once-proud nation of Moldo-va, but they weren't on my route. I had never put Botoșani on my list of attractive Moldovan cities but now I realise that there is something magical about the place. But this doesn't make sense as Botoșani is the ultimate provincial one-horse town – small, parochial, industrialised and ugly – and people in the bigger cities of the region like to look down on it. Even the people living there don't seem to like it. I went to the bank and there was a long queue of de-pressed looking people; and if you meet any young people they'll tell you, in fluent English, that they can't wait to em-igrate to Western Europe. But there's a lot more to Botoșani than their empty factories and queues might suggest. Apart from anything else, everyone I came across was extremely helpful. This had been a big Jewish market town before the Second World War, an important commercial centre, and also the birthplace of some of Romania's greatest cultural icons: the national poet, Eminescu, the celebrated composer, Enescu, and Iorga, the polymath historian who's been described as Romania's Voltaire.

Many Romanian cities have a small, old, picturesque centre which is surrounded by hectares of ghastly concrete blocks. What makes a Romanian city is what they do with the old centre. In Sibiu and Braşov they have restored them well, but there are plenty of other cities that have failed to do this. Botoşani's old centre really isn't much to write home about and, when I was there, it was a building site with a big EU subsidy sign but no sign of any actual work going on. But there are boulevards which are lined with huge trees and beautiful old buildings, plenty of young people who haven't yet emigrated and all this gave off an atmosphere that I found charming and exotic. The quiet, the fresh air and the people all conspired to make me feel positive and energetic.

My conclusion is that the more remote and forgotten a Romanian town or village is, the more attractive it is. It confirms my experience that the more unpopular a place is, the more friendly the people tend to be. Ever since seeing the Romanian villages in 1990 I have wanted to live in one, but the question is what would I do? How could I make a living? We can enjoy these places from a superficial point of view, or on a short visit, but I've never worked out how to actually live there [postscript: and now that the UK has crashed out of the EU I need a visa to stay in Romania for more than three months]. Back in the early 1990s I did actually live in a village, near Botoşani, when renovating a children's home. But that's another story.

# MISSION IMPOSSIBLE: BRANDING ROMANIA

A lot of money is being invested into the development of a brand for Romania, resulting in embarrassment and financial loss. Branding a country requires a level of coordination and trust that is unattainable in Romania. According to Charles Brymer, chairman of Interbrand, "Creating a brand program for a country demands an integration policy that most countries do not possess – the ability to act and speak in a coordinated and repetitive way."

The word branding has a somewhat violent origin in the English language. A brand is a metal symbol, or number, on the end of an iron rod, that marks ownership over cattle. The brand would be heated until red and then stamped onto the hapless cow. Somehow the term got transferred to businesses where a company can represent its philosophy, or underlying idea, if it has one, by developing a particular look and ensuring that it's replicated in everything they do. Branding sounds simple and many advertising agencies offer this service, even though they often fail to realise that it's more than just a slogan and a logo and, as a result, it tends to be only the big corporations that get branding right: Not only can they afford the top branding consultants but they have the internal discipline to enforce the visual guidelines throughout their empires.

How many nations have actually succeeded in developing a brand? Very few. Scotland, Ireland and New Zealand are credited with success in this field but all of these countries are, according to Charles Brymer, "clever and small". He also says they had a positive image to start with and were able to involve the public in the process. Getting the population involved in a national brand development process is, apparently, an essential requirement for success and this is the one guarantee that it will never happen in

Romania – where even political allies can barely agree on anything. I don't believe it actually happened in my own country, Scotland, and when I looked at our official branding page, on Scotland.org, I found words that are, for me, meaningless and uninspiring: "Brand Scotland tells the authentic story of Scotland as a bold and positive country, rich in history and heritage but moving forward in a way that is progressive, pioneering and inclusive." Whenever I see the word authentic used in marketing or PR I want to reach for the sick bag.

Countries like France, Italy and the USA are already so well known, and so full of tourists, that they just don't need a brand. In 1996 the British government pumped out a Cool Britannia slogan to take advantage of the dynamic pop culture of the era, but government involvement was the kiss of death and their attempt at using it for national branding was ridiculed by the media. However, all these countries are good at promoting themselves, dealing with the media, protecting their image and burying inconvenient truths. Most of them have come to the rather obvious conclusion that they simply don't need a brand.

What Romania needs to do is improve its image abroad. This is an essential requirement in order to increase foreign investment and tourism – both of which are essential for modern economic development. There are three essential steps involved in this: addressing the negatives, improving the points of access and city centres, and understanding the mentality of the foreign visitor. But these requirements aren't taken seriously in Romania, and as a result there is no change in their negative international image. These issues could be addressed relatively easily and would cost a lot less than trying to develop a national brand.

Many Romanians blame the Roma minority for their negative image abroad, but this can be addressed by simply admitting that there is a problem with discrimination against this minority, and by presenting the progress made by the Ministry of Education in getting Roma kids into schools. Apparently Romania has the most Roma teachers in Europe, each one of whom is charged with helping Roma kids integrate into school – and getting them into the school system is one of the ways that this marginalised population can be given the same opportunities as the rest of the Romanian people. I think that most foreign visitors to Romania don't see the Roma problem in Romania but may well complain about foreign Roma begging in their own nations. I think foreigners are more offended by what they see at Bucharest airport: outrageously massive banner advertising, gridlock, and new buildings which are an offence to the eye. Even before they leave the airport, visitors have to push their way through a mob of overweight, aggressive taxi drivers and if they get to Bucharest's main railway station the impression gets worse as this is where the city's tramps and street addicts congregate.

Charles Brymer says that the best impressions of foreign visitors are formed at the points of access and the city centres – and Romania fails badly on both counts. I have entered Romania by road from Serbia, Bulgaria, Hungary and Ukraine and the impression at all these points is of chaos, litter scattered by the wind, and buildings which are either grey, huge and derelict or brand new with blue roofs and silver windows. Lara, my daughter-editor said, "You're not even spared the pain when you're on the plane because, if you look down, all the silver tin roofs will blind you."

Other than exceptions like Sibiu and Timișoara, many of Romania's city centres consist of brutalist, concrete architecture. The visual damage caused by uncontrolled building and banner advertising is one thing, but what bothers many visitors is that it is not possible to walk on the pavements of Bucharest as they are full of parked cars – something that is illegal in most EU cities.

The final recommendation for country branding is to listen to foreign tourists and, as far as I can see, Romania has failed on this front too. I've never seen a study along these lines but I've always hoped to play a role in creating a national brand, as I'm a foreigner, I work in PR and have lots of ideas about how Romania could be promoted abroad. I even met a Romanian Minister of Tourism and tried to suggest that she could think about targeting niche groups of foreigners, such as bird watchers, eco tourists, mountain bikers, hikers, people who like camping (people like me!) rather than putting all their eggs in one basket and always chasing the bloated, elderly, mass tourist from Germany who just wants to get roasted on overcrowded beaches. Why not promote the traditional Romanian villages and all the wonders of rural Transylvania and Moldova. I wasn't able to say half of this as the minister was dismissive and didn't want to listen. I was subsequently asked to evaluate 12 different ideas that were being developed by the creatives at a leading advertising agency. They were pitching for a multi-million euro tender, put out by the Ministry of Tourism, for international TV spots to promote Romania abroad. Although the creatives at this ad agency were young and hip, and all spoke fluent English, their ideas were completely rotten and I didn't rate any of them as having any chance abroad. The main problem I saw was that all these concepts were just highlighting the most beautiful things about Romania – mountains, castles and women – without trying to address any of the negatives. My suggestion of tackling the negatives head on by stating, for example, *you might have thought Romania was a dump but check out these great things…* was dismissed out of hand.

The best example of a failed attempt to brand Romania was the campaign conducted in 2010 by Elena Udrea, the Minister for Tourism at the time. The branding slogan that emerged was Explore the Carpathian Garden, a confusing phrase considering the Carpathians are a mountain range and not a garden. But it was the logo, a green leaf, which caused the real scandal in Romania: Not only was the image available online for $250, it had already been used by a Romanian chemical factory and the British public campaign Change Transport. Needless to say, this campaign made absolutely no headway internationally despite the millions of euros that had been thrown at it. Eight years later Elena Udrea was sentenced to prison on corruption charges – she fled to Costa Rica but came back a year later and is still serving time for what she did in government.

If the simple branding advice noted above could be taken into consideration, and effective national branding could happen, Romania could become a nicer place to visit, as the train stations and entry points would be cleaned up, and the most effective impact of all would come into play – word of mouth promotion. Imagine the impact of one foreigner telling another that Romania is a good place to visit and that the old image of it being a hellhole is no longer valid.

# BUREAUCRATS BAN ANCIENT RURAL PRACTICES

The proposed ban against transhumance is symptomatic of
the Romanian government's attitude towards people living
in rural areas, and it goes against the values of the EU –
which genuinely tries to support traditional practices like
this. But what the hell, you might ask, quite reasonably, is
transhumance? It's the ancient practice of taking huge flocks
of sheep to mountain pastures for the summer and back
down in the winter, where they get returned to their individual owners and given shelter. The deal between the owners
of the individual sheep, the villager, and the shepherd is that
the animals are loaned to the shepherd for the hot seasons,
taken to the mountains where the grazing is good, and protected from wild animals, wolves and bears, by huge dogs
that accompany the flocks. The shepherds make a living by
milking the sheep and making cheese which would then be
sold in local markets. The owners of the individual sheep
would get a share of these profits, which were considerable
under communism when there was a chronic food shortage in Romania. Transhumance was practised in the UK
many centuries ago, before agriculture was taken over by
machines, and it's a wonder that it's still being done in the
Balkan nations of southeast Europe. Another thing that you,
the reader, may not be aware of is that Romania has been
part of the EU since 2007.

Transhumance not only offers employment in the countryside, where jobs are rare and emigration high, but it's
also of real interest to the growing number of people who
are interested in environmentally friendly lifestyles: you can
now join these shepherds in their great hikes across mountain ranges but, I assume, you'd need a lot of travel experience to be able to handle it – not only the relentless walking
but dealing with these gruff shepherds can't be easy. I've

also been told, by a Romanian friend, Sorina Stallard, who read this manuscript, that transhumance is "at the heart of a whole network of cultural and traditional practices that span the crafts, music, poetry, painting, photography, tourism, gastronomy, religion and identity".

I worked on a lot of EU-funded projects, especially before 2007 when Romania was invited to join the bloc. Prior to this date the EU pumped a lot of money into helping the Romanians adapt their legal framework to be closer to those of the other EU member states. As you can imagine this was a complicated and messy process in all of the former communist countries of Eastern Europe; you can't just sweep under the carpet all those years of communist, and imperial, tyranny. You can change the laws easily enough but it takes generations to change behaviour. And what's becoming ever more apparent is that the suspicion, fear and cynicism that communism instilled in their subjects is now re-emerging as conspiracy theories and extreme nationalism. To cut a long story short, I was a cog in this machine of change and it's relevant here as I was witness to some really interesting conversations, between foreign consultants and the Romanian government officials they were working with.

One of the things I picked up was that the Romanian government blindly agreed to the conditions that came with EU membership, without first checking if they fit the Romanian context and culture. Part of the EU Accession Process is that each Candidate Country has the opportunity to challenge, change, ignore or adapt individual pieces of EU law, according to their own national context. But this requires study, analysis, communication, the formation of official positions – in other words a lot of hassle for a government that tends to just wave new laws through without much concern for the details or its impact. I worked with one British consultant who, like me, was working with a Romanian government department and being funded by an

EU grant – hundreds of so-called experts from EU nations were working alongside Romanian officials, trying to help them modernise the way they worked. My colleague had been working in Poland, which joined the EU in 2004, before coming to Romania. He told me how the Polish Government had refused to follow the EU norm of applying visas to neighbouring Ukraine, as there was a huge flow of migrant labour that Poland relied on economically. They negotiated an exception to the rules and Ukrainian citizens continued coming to Poland without visas. This is how a small part of the global brain drain works – the infamous Polish Plumber would move to the UK, where he was made famous by the tabloid newspapers, while his Ukrainian counterpart took his place in Poland.

Romania, by contrast, spoiled its relationship with Serbia, Moldova and Turkey by meekly applying the EU visa rules without any attempt to negotiate on behalf of its neighbours. Adrian Năstase, Romania's Prime Minister at the time, was desperate to claim the credit for getting Romania into the EU and to his credit, he succeeded: on January the 1st 2007 Romania was invited to join the world's biggest economic bloc. Năstase had ridden roughshod over the ministries in getting into the EU and had told them to not bother negotiating all those pesky little details that should have been adapted for the Romanian context. Five years later, in 2012, Adrian Năstase was sentenced to two years in prison for corruption.

It's clear to those of us who have worked with Romanian government officials that they have little respect for people living in the countryside. Just look at the neglected schools in Romania's villages – most of the resources for non-university education go to the top schools in each of the county capitals and it's an unofficial policy that rural schools, and especially those with a Roma majority, just don't matter. The fact that over thirty percent of Romania's population live in the countryside does not seem to be a concern for the policymakers in Bucharest. Why don't they invest in these kids? Surely they will become Romania's future workforce? What happens if it becomes economically impossible to survive in the village? What if millions of peasants come to the cities, expecting jobs that they will never qualify for, asking for social assistance and housing? None of these scenarios seem to be under consideration. [2023 Postscript: this problem was solved by mass emigration to other EU nations where these hard-working villagers were welcomed and put to work. I just saw a statistic which says that about thirty percent of Romanians have emigrated and this would suggest that the villages are now empty].

During this time I met a geeky-looking British guy (skinny, scruffy red hair, badly dressed) who had been hired by the World Bank to advise Romania's Ministry of Agriculture. He told me about a conversation he'd had at the ministry with an official. My geeky pal asked the official what their policy on subsistence farmers was. The official looked blank for a while and then said, sotto voce, "Don't worry, the rural population are poor and old. Soon they will be dead and there will be no more problem."

He also told me how subsistence farmers are counted in the Ministry of Agriculture's official surveys. He explained that normal members of the population have certain numbers that show how much money they contribute to the economy – in other words, their income. Even unemployed people make a financial contribution in these surveys as they get welfare payments which end up being spent in the economy. "But next to the list of people living off the land," he explained, "is a blank. No numbers, no financial contribution to the economy …". I didn't understand and asked him to explain. He said that because subsistence farmers, or peasants, grow their own food and have their own animals, they're self-sufficient and economically independent from the State. They simply don't fit into the modern economic systems that we've constructed around ourselves and the results of this are tragic: if the value of the rural population isn't recognised by Romania's government then, obviously, there will be no investment in sustaining these lifestyles. Not only will schools and rural infrastructure be neglected but it will become increasingly hard to survive in a village, and there will be no incentives for new people to move in. The final solution, presumably, will be the selling of Romania's high-quality farming land to investors for mechanised farming.

But isn't being self-sufficient a great thing? Isn't that what we should be aspiring to? Wouldn't it be great to be living off the land and not relying on a job with an international company? Couldn't this be an option in a modern economy? In my view yes, but in the view of the agricultural experts – no. It seems there is a consensus that the subsistence farmer, not to mention the shepherd, is a statistical anomaly, an unproductive element of our urban-based economy, and they need to be swept away. This is what happened in my own country, the UK, and it would be tragic if Romania makes the same mistake as these people, these villagers, are the repository of ancient traditions and indigenous culture. I personally admire their way of life. If the Romanian government were to decide that the welfare of the rural population is a concern, EU funds could be assigned to developing all sorts of projects that would support these ancient lifestyles, as well as traditional practices like transhumance. But it would need to be done sensitively so that the small farmer, the individual, isn't swept away by the usual beneficiary of EU grants – big business. Considering how complicated the EU grant application process is and the need for a consultant, like me, to apply for it and then monitor it, the best way to approach this would be for the county authorities to design projects to improve rural infrastructure: schools, clinics, roads, utilities, renewable energy, micro-loans, communal storage and transport facilities. They could provide the support services needed to support small-scale subsistence farming.

The French have been very good at getting EU money to their farmers. They apparently get about a quarter of the EU's Common Agricultural Policy loot – worth over fifty billion euros – and there are interesting examples from all over the EU of how traditional and modern lifestyles are supported in the countryside. One example is from the Highlands of Scotland, an area that was so depopulated that it seems almost empty. With the help of EU funds, the British government invested in new telecommunication lines, internet and business centres in villages – what they call Tele Cottages – and young wealthy people from London started relocating to the Highlands. However, only two percent of the British population live in the countryside and many people, like me, are sad that we have lost many of our traditions as a result of generations of urbanisation. But now that awareness of global warming is rising there is, I hope, more interest in rural lifestyles. When Britons visit Romania, we're enchanted by the villages. It's a way of life that some of us appreciate more than Romanians do, a fact that often bewilders our Romanian hosts. We've lost it in the West, and it would be a shame for it to fade into non-existence in Romania as well. There are so many ways it could be saved, if only the government gave a damn.

## Postscript

I published this story in 2008, a year after Romania had joined the EU. The situation has changed dramatically since then and the people I have asked about the proposed transhumance ban don't even remember it. Fortunately, it wasn't banned. This story is, by journalistic standards, grossly out of date. Again, the same question: Why include it? The answer is that it gives an insight into how Romania's central government regards their rural population, and I'm quite sure these attitudes apply to this day. It's also a snapshot about how Romania's integration into the EU worked out just after it had joined the bloc. If I was to write a story now, about rural practices and the EU, it would be totally different and probably all about corruption and land erosion. I think it offers a valuable insight into a moment of Romania's development.

When I posted this story on my blog back in 2008 I got a really interesting comment from someone whose description of transhumance is so lyrical that it serves as a useful complement to what I wrote about it. The comment was posted by a French lady called Métilde Wendenbaum: "All over Europe, in late spring and early summer, countless sheep, goats and cows perform a sort of carefully choreographed dance as they move northwards from parched plains to greener pastures and alpine meadows. The annual transhumance has begun.

"In Autumn, the herders traditionally move back their flocks from high pastures to their winter quarters on the plains. In Bulgaria, and all over the Balkans, sheep were moved for centuries. But this tradition has been lost due to the pressure of modernization. A key player in the transhumance revival in Bulgaria is Emilian Stoynov from the Fund for Wild Fauna and Flora. His team strives to restore long-distance transhumance due to its importance for grassland habitats. They organise tours for hikers to accompany shepherd's families and up to 600 sheep. Although there are bears and wolves in Bulgaria there's no need to be scared because Karakachan dogs accompany us."

# ROMANIA'S MONTY PYTHON INSTITUTIONS

Getting into one of Romania's public institutions is like banging the door of a mediaeval castle in a Monty Python film. If you approach one of the many state institutions in Bucharest several beefy guards will appear, block the entrance, ask what you want, demand identification, and send you packing if you look too lowly or happen to be a member of the Roma minority. Their job is to keep people out. The comparison with western institutions is stark: in other EU Member States you are greeted by well-informed staff who do their best to handle your request, give you contact details and offer you leaflets and brochures. They might even show you into a seating area. You leave feeling as if they understand that a public institution actually needs some interaction with the public.

The thugs guarding Romania's vast institutions – whose purposes are vague but costs are huge – make you feel that you have disturbed their boozy chat, or snooze, and that you have absolutely no right to enter their sacrosanct ministry or embassy – the Ministry of Foreign Affairs extensive network of foreign properties. One of the many bizarre facts about this Balkan country is that it has some of the most fabulous embassies on the planet. In London, Romania owns a huge Victorian town house opposite Prince Charles' palace. In New York they own a whole block in downtown Manhattan, and in Rome they have a couple of grand palaces. Most of these splendid buildings were bought by Romania's kings, before the Second World War, and seem to serve no purpose, at least in the case of the Italian palaces, beyond providing accommodation for retired Romanian diplomats and their extended families.

Some time ago I visited Romania's Embassy in France, a small and exquisite palace in a smart district of Paris – a stone's throw from the Eiffel Tower. There was a 1980s buzzer on the ancient door and I asked for the cultural attaché in my bad French. *Poff teats?* (Excuse me? in Romanian) shouted back an angry voice, presumably outraged that he'd been disturbed from his slumbers in a language he didn't understand. I switched to the Romanian language and convinced the sceptical guard that I wasn't a dirty peasant or, God forbid, a member of the Roma minority, but a serious professional who had an appointment with the cultural attaché. After some time a door opened and a grumpy brute in a shabby blue suit reluctantly let me in, before shuffling back to his lair. The cultural attaché was as different from the glowering, monosyllabic guard as was possible to be. He was well-educated, charming, multilingual and fascinating. He showed me around the palace and told me they couldn't afford to renovate it – especially the small theatre that would cost fifteen million euros to repair – and that soon he'd be off to Morocco as Romania's new ambassador. Romania's diplomats are often like this. They glide effortlessly between international postings, NATO missions, summit meetings and the EU institutions. They form part of Romania's ruling class, alongside the gaudy new millionaire-politicians. A Romanian reader of this manuscript asked if "all diplomats are like this," and I'm sure they're not, these are just my impressions. The point I'm trying to make here is that the contrast between these smooth patricians, and the brutes that keep the public out of Romania's public institutions, is much starker than in the west and closer to the Monty Python parodies.

When these diplomats enter public institutions in Romania the suspicious guards stand to attention as if the commander-in-chief is visiting, and wave them through. They ignore the rules of access that are so strictly applied to the rest of the population. Even though these guards can be intimidating, they in turn can be easily intimidated. All it takes is a whiff of the arrogance of the ruling class. Well-dressed foreign visitors to Bucharest can be treated with this fawning reverence and, as a foreigner, you can get into a Romanian institution if you brandish your passport with the right level of arrogance. The right clothing is as important as the attitude and if they get one whiff of the western traveller, or, in my case, a penniless writer, you'll be out on your ear. When I would walk into these places I was working as an EU consultant to various Romanian ministries so I did have the right attitude and probably came across as arrogant. Now, I have no intention of trying to get into those institutions again.

The ruling class in Romania, and in many other former communist countries, seem to regard ordinary people as an ignorant herd that needs to be treated like cattle – and kept out of the public institutions at all costs – and public policy is made accordingly. Communicating with public institutions is complex and their websites are often incomprehensible. The aim of these websites is, in my opinion, to show how sophisticated they are and not to inform the public. A Frenchman once told me an expression from his country that applies to Romania: "Why make it simple when you can keep it complicated?"

In the west you can contact an institution by writing a letter, email, or even phoning up – but in Romania you must go to the institution and stand in a line with other hapless supplicants.

When you get to the head of the queue you must bow down, as if to complete your humiliation, and speak through a tiny hatch in the wall to the foul-tempered official on the other side. More often than not they will then send you to another institution, or a room on the fifth floor, in order to get your document stamped. Often you then have to go to some obscure cashier, hand over a small amount of money and get some official stamps. Not only does all this waste an incredible amount of people's time but it causes an endless amount of stress. No wonder the Romanians complain about their bureaucracy.

When writing this article I came across a Romanian environmentalist called Raul Cazan and discussed this issue with him. He told me about Pierre Bourdieu, a French sociologist, anthropologist, philosopher and public intellectual. Cazan gave me a theoretical explanation of bureaucracy that makes a lot of sense: "Bourdieu sees bureaucracy as an actual organism, independent of individuals. In Romania, public administration is literally a cancer on local development. It can carry out some public works such as paving the streets or insulation of buildings; nevertheless, innovation lacks completely. Kitsch and stupidity rule. Romanian society is so deeply corrupt that you feel its stench at every level in the public administration."

I find this idea of Pierre Bourdieu really compelling – bureaucracy is a monster that needs constant feeding, rather like the Aztecs needed a constant supply of human victims to sacrifice to their gods. But I don't agree with Cazan that Romanian society is irredeemably corrupt. There is corruption at every level in Romania, and the system *is* dysfunctional, but I've worked with a lot of public servants in EU projects and they all seemed bright, young and eager to learn. Never have any of them tried to offer me a bribe or asked for some kind of favour. There are good people in every institution, trying to make things work – but unfortunately these people are hidden away on the inside and when it comes to the big decision makers, the men at the top, I believe it's quite another story.

An example of the dysfunctionality of the system can be seen every day on the streets of Bucharest where cars are allowed to park all over the pavements, forcing everyone from young mothers, children and old people, to walk onto the main road in order to pass. In other words, car owners have more rights than pedestrians – a reality that has no basis in the Christian values that all Romanian leaders supposedly believe in. The worst thing about this car-parking-on-the-pavements problem is that everyone seems to think that treating cars as superior is normal and nothing can be done to change it. I've had endless conversations with taxi drivers, pedestrians and Romanian friends about it and they all tell me the driver's viewpoint: there's nowhere to park, the city council should provide more parking spaces, what can the poor drivers do? It seems that the victims of this practice are on the side of the perpetrators.

The best way to describe public official attitudes to the common people in Romania is to refer to a scene in one of the best films ever made by Terry Gilliam and the Monty Python team: *Time Bandits*. This romp through time passes through mediaeval England and at one point the hapless Time Bandits, a bunch of dwarves, meet up with Robin Hood and his Merry Men – a bunch of thugs led by an aristocrat. Robin Hood is played by John Cleese who takes on the persona of the Duke of Edinburgh, repeating the same meaningless pleasantries to everyone: "Well done! Jolly, jolly good! Is that so? Really? Ha, ha, ha!" The dwarves (our heroes) are lined up with the mediaeval peasants to shake hands with the Great Robin Hood. After Mr. Hood says a few inane words to everyone in the queue, a hulking henchman punches each hapless peasant in the head and they fall to the ground. After a spate of this pointless violence John Cleese asks the henchman "Is that really necessary?" and the henchman grunts back in the affirmative. The Duke of Edinburgh character shrugs and says something like "Alright then". It's just the way things were done and nobody can change it.

I've been based in Romania for some time and whenever I have to go to a public institution I imagine that I must blag my way into a mediaeval fortress. I switch from being an ordinary person on the street into an arrogant foreigner, and this attitude gives me the posture and look that I need to impress the guards. It also makes life more interesting than it would be in London, as I must put on roles and behave in ways I would never do back home. The saving grace about Romania is that the people are friendly and helpful, even those guarding the institutions. Once you get past their initial hostility, you realise that there's a friendly person underneath all that gruffness.

But it's not only in Romania where the institutions are like this. Many years ago I met an American army officer in Bosnia-Herzegovina who told me that he would sometimes use a packet of Marlboro to get into the Pentagon, where he used to work. "It's all about attitude," he said, "I would look at the guards with impatience and arrogance, flash my fake ID, the packet of Marlboro, bark some military jargon … and it worked every time!" I subsequently told this story to an American friend who worked for the US Air Force and he said: "That must have been pre-9/11. That guy would be arrested if he tried that nowadays." This made me think, when did that conversation take place with the American officer in Bosnia? Hmm … it would have been in 1996 or 1997, in other words just a few years before the 9/11 terrorist attack changed everything. Even now, so many years later, that conversation remains fresh in my memory: I love it when the pompous, brittle sheen of authority is punctured, or shown to be useless.

## Postscript

Needless to say this article is hopelessly out of date but, as with the others, still relevant. It's now March 2023 and I'm back in Romania where I've seen plenty of gruff, overweight, hostile looking guards outside public institutions. Fortunately I have no need to behave like a pig and try to get in. Now I'm writing books and helping people with their homes. Lara, my daughter-editor, added this comment to the manuscript when she edited it: "It's not just institutions. It's everywhere. Customer service is atrocious. There are some who are really nice, but the majority of people who work in any sort of position that involves dealing with the public act as if dealing with you is some sort of awful punishment enacted by a vengeful god. And they all have a sour look on their faces. I could just go up to the till in a coffee shop and ask for a coffee and they'll glare at me like I just stole their firstborn child."

# I WAS WRONG ABOUT THE ROMA MINORITY

For many years I thought I knew the answer to the problems faced by the Roma minority: education. If school was more appealing to this population their situation of marginalisation would gradually end, and they would learn the skills needed to challenge the discrimination they are faced with all over Europe. A new book I just read made me realise that there's no simple answer to Roma poverty, and that I know a lot less than I assumed about the Roma population. It made me ask myself if I'm nothing more than an arrogant, patronising know-it-all? The book I'm referring to is called *I Met Lucky People: The Story of the Romani Gypsies,* by Yaron Matras, and it's incredible. I agree with the quotes on the cover: The Financial Times says it is "required reading" (I would add *for government officials and teachers across Europe*) and The Sunday Times is quoted as saying, "Almost everything we imagine we know about Gypsies is wrong."

This book challenges my own view of the Roma which has been formed in opposition to what most Romanians I've met have said. Many Romanians seem infuriated by the fact that certain members of the Roma minority can be seen begging in city centres across Europe, bringing their country into disrepute. When I point out that this is only a small percentage of the Roma population they dismiss me as naive. The fact that many of these beggars, in my experience at least, don't say they come from Romania, perhaps because their whole country has a bad reputation, isn't known in Romania. These same people blame Romania's poor international image on the Roma, while claiming that they're not in the slightest bit racist – many people I've spoken with genuinely believe that hating the Roma has nothing to do with racism. Other complaints are that the Roma don't follow the basic rules of society, starting with obligatory school attendance through to their apparent reluctance to do normal jobs. The other stereotypes I've heard in Romania since 1990 is that the Roma don't want to go to school, they can't work and they all steal, and from what I've heard in other European countries I think these views are shared across the continent. In an attempt to address these particular prejudices I made a documentary film called *The Land is Waiting,* with Laurențiu Calciu, about a large Roma family in a village in north-east Romania, in which they were all working the land and going to school or university. Another problem is that the Roma are not good at promoting themselves and are often rejected by the more prominent and better integrated minorities.

What's now clear to me is that the Roma are grossly misunderstood and this new book gives us the opportunity to gain insight into their culture, come to terms with the fact that we have a common history and work out how to tolerate each other better. Let's start with education. I had assumed the problem was with the majority population not wanting Roma kids in their schools and discriminating against them if they do get in. This is certainly part of the problem and, in Romania at least, the State itself discriminates against Roma kids by allocating the least resources to the schools where there is a Roma majority. They also tolerate the practice of school administrators telling Roma families that there is no place for them. This routine practice, which is always done verbally, so there are no written records, keeps Roma kids out of Romania's top schools. There are positive discrimination processes in place, to reserve places in public schools and universities, but I know one girl who got into a top Bucharest school, without having the appropriate results, by claiming to be Roma.

But I wasn't fully aware of the Roma perspective and this is where the new book helps. This is what the author,

Yaron Matras, writes about education: "Traditional Roma families educate their children by allowing them to participate in all family activities. Children observe, join in and gradually assume a share of responsibility for the extended household. There is no initiation ceremony and no formal testing of acquired skills or knowledge …. School is seen as a Gadje (non-Romani) institution. It represents everything that outsiders stand for and everything that separates Roma from outsiders: rigid rules; obedience towards a person in authority who is not part of the family; oppression of children's own initiative and spontaneous and open expression of emotion; withholding of responsibility from children; imposition of arbitrary schedules; and, perhaps the most difficult of all, separation of children from the rest of the family for long hours."

Matras builds a portrait of Roma family life and several things seem impressive: their ancient system of holding families together, sharing responsibility among an extended family, the key role of old people as leaders and also child-minders; their complex rules of washing and hygiene; their freelance work ethic; the fact that they involve children in everything. Their history is interesting and the fact that their language has remained active after a thousand years on the road, not to mention the oppression, is quite remarkable.

I really like their approach to education which is to keep their children close at all times and teach them everything they know; the boys learn traditional trades from the men and the girls learn domestic skills as well as the mother's profession, such as selling goods at market. Even though begging is frowned on by most Roma families, it's considered as work and those who do it don't try to hide it from their children. Among themselves they are scrupulously honest and they have their own system of conflict resolution, in the form of consensus-based Roma courts known as *Kris*. I can relate to all this. For the first ten years of my school life, I couldn't understand what the hell I was doing there and the only explanation I came up with was that I'm stupid. I would have been much happier just hanging around at home, in the woods and the river, learning from my parents. I think it's unnatural to separate kids from their parents for their formative years. The most valuable things I learned in life, and am still learning, were from my own mistakes.

Although I was wrong about the Roma when it comes to education and I was woefully ignorant of their culture, despite much exposure to it in Romania, I do have an open mind and am keen to learn more and understand them better. I try not to be judgemental or make generalisations as these are almost always wrong; but this is so hard as making generalisations is fun and it makes me feel clever. All I can say about the Roma gypsies and their educational needs is I don't know. I used to think I knew the answer – education – but now I know that I don't. As a society, in Romania as well as in my own country, I think we need to approach the Roma minority without an agenda, we should listen to them, understand them better, genuinely respect their culture and accommodate their requests. We should ask what they need for their children's education, what ideas for education they have, take their replies seriously and consider re-assigning some of the resources we put into mainstream schools. If we really want to address their marginalisation we could, initially just by listening. Surely it's wrong to impose our values and structures on the Roma people and then condemn them for not complying?

# ARGUING ABOUT THE WORD ROMA

Romania's government caused outrage among Roma organisations after it asked Parliament to accept a proposal to change the official name of the Roma minority from *Roma*, which means man in the Roma language, to Tzigane, which comes from the Greek term for untouchable. The government said the name change is necessary because of the possible confusion among the international community between the words Roma – which refers to the Roma / gypsy ethnic minority – and Romania, a nation proud of its historical status as a part of the Roman Empire. Romanians are rightly proud of the fact that they survived, speaking a form of Latin, in a hostile part of Europe which was overrun by wave after wave of eastern invaders such as the Hungarians. This country is sometimes called a Latin island in a sea of Slavs, and the fact it survived as an ethnic group for so long is impressive. Meanwhile, the Romanian Academy, whose role is to protect Romanian culture and language, supported the name change on the grounds that many countries in the European Union use a variation of the word Tzigane to refer to their Roma populations.

"Imagine if a U.S. Congressman proposed to change the name Afro-American back to the insulting term n_____," said David Mark, director of the Roma Civic Alliance in Bucharest. "It would cause a huge scandal and that Congressman would probably have to resign." The controversial legislation was put forward by maverick lawmaker Silviu Prigoană, a member of Romania's ruling Liberal Democratic Party, who claimed he was acting on behalf of several Roma groups from Transylvania who, he claimed, "don't like to use the word Roma." I went to meet him in his kitsch office in southern Bucharest and asked him to provide the names of these groups. But Prigoană couldn't, saying only that they are "those gypsy fellows in Transylvania who wear the big hats" – presumably meaning the Hungarian-speaking Roma groups who go by the collective name of Gabor. His rationale for the Roma groups support of the name-change was so scanty that I wondered if he'd just made it up. I was also surprised that the Romanian media didn't make more of this weak link in his argument.

Prigoană denied the suggestion that he was acting on the orders of Romania's canny President, Traian Băsescu, which is what many people suspected at the time. The president had stated on public radio that the introduction of the politically correct term Roma, in 1995, at the recommendation of Romania's Foreign Ministry, was "a big mistake." The President went on to say, "Many Europeans are confused by the terms Roma and Romania. They wonder if it is an ethnicity or a nation of 22 million citizens." The government has never made any attempt to explain the difference between the words – probably because Romanians would rather not be associated with the Roma minority at all. If I was in power I'd initiate a big public awareness campaign that celebrated the Roma culture and that Romania is celebrating, not hiding, the fact that they're a big minority in Romania. Not only would this make it clear that the Roma are a minority, clearing up that confusion some foreigners have that the Roma and the Romanians are the same thing, but it would put Romania on track to join those other nations that embrace their multiculturalism: Australia, Canada, France, Germany, and the USA. The big advantage of multiculturalism in general, and embracing the Roma population in particular, is demographic: immigrants and minorities increase the population numbers in all those nations mentioned above, and Romania's population is in freefall so surely it makes sense to properly support and educate the Roma minority. In Romania there are an estimated two million Roma people even though a lot of them don't declare themselves as such in the census for fear of persecution. There's also a lot of ethnic Hungarians in Romania, around one and a half million.

According to Romani Criss, a leading Roma organisation in Bucharest, the government never consulted with representatives of the Roma minority about the proposed name change. But the right of minorities to choose their own name is enshrined in international law, and so the Romanian government is creating future problems in terms of a human rights backlash. "Self-determination is the right of a people to determine its own destiny," reads the Council of Europe's Convention for the Protection of National Minorities. In a protest letter sent to the Organization for Security and Cooperation in Europe (OSCE), 24 Roma groups stated that the name Tzigane "is associated in the collective memory of the Roma with the slavery that existed in Romania from 1385 to 1856, and also the forced deportations in WW2." The OSCE had already criticised Romania for trying to classify its Roma minority as Tzigane once before, in 1995.

Unfortunately the Romanian public supports the name change, at least they did at the time of writing, and many resent the Roma for the bad press stemming from the forced deportations out of France and other western European countries. Observers fear the seemingly minor issue of a name change could unleash a new wave of discrimination. "The proposal is a matter of concern as it would reinforce old stereotypes and prejudice," wrote Andrzej Mirga, head of the OSCE's Contact Point for Roma Issues. "It would also be inconsistent with Romania's international obligations. The preferences of the Roma in Romania as to how they want to be referred to should be respected. After all [the use of the word Roma] was a conscious political decision precisely to move away from stereotypes equating Tzigane with crime [and] poverty."

Madga Matache, the director of Romani Criss, told me,

"We are speaking to our lawyers, working on legal challenges to the Romanian Academy, and we are talking to OSCE and the Council of Europe, who I am sure will support us in this struggle." Roma groups lobbied Parliament in Bucharest, while activists started a worldwide petition against the legislation to send to Romania's government. With the dignity of the Romany people at stake, as well as Romania's international reputation for human rights, a lot was riding on the outcome of this semantic clash.

## Postscript

This story was published by Time Magazine in 2010, one of three articles I published with that magazine. The bill to drop the name Roma came to nothing but the underlying issue of discrimination against the Roma minority is still unresolved in Romania. But mass Roma emigration to Western Europe has decreased the size of the minority and also, I suspect, removed the most active of the Roma leaders. Something else happened at the time that's worth mentioning here: the term ROM was quietly dropped from Romanian passports – every country has a three-letter country code – and it was replaced with ROU, a term that comes from, I presume, Roumania, which is the French word for the nation. Also, the nation had been called Roumania before the communists took over in 1946 and imposed the name: the Socialist Republic of Romania.

# ROMANIA: THE WORLD'S FIRST DYSTOPIA

A dystopia is a nightmare vision of the future and there are two great books which have defined the genre: *1984* and *Brave New World*. Both books are brilliant but they were written in the 1930s when the world quivered under the shadow of totalitarianism. They're useful for understanding the 20th Century but outdated when it comes to our own troubled times. Now we have an author, David Mitchell, who has projected the economics of today hundreds of years into the future. We also have a country – Romania – where a Canadian mining company is planning a vast cyanide mining project that would fit nicely into Mr. Mitchell's dystopia.

This is how David Mitchell describes the future in his breathtaking novel, *Cloud Atlas:* "Its soil is polluted, its rivers lifeless, its air toxloaded, its food supplies riddled with rogue genes. The downstrata can't buy the drugs necessary to counter these privations. Melanoma and malaria belts advance northwards at 40 kilometres per year. Those production zones of Africa and Indonesia that supply Consumer Zones' demands are 60% uninhabitable. Plutocracy's legitimacy, its wealth, is drying up …. Its only response is that strategy beloved by all bankrupt ideologues: denial.

It's not hard to see how today's multinationals could evolve into the monopolies described by Mitchell. The scandals regarding the non-tax-paying antics of companies like Starbucks, Google and Apple suggest that the main role of modern government is to represent big business. What this means in practice is that the interests of big business will always trump those of ordinary people or the environment. The process can be seen clearly in an emerging economy like Romania, a country that has been a capitalist economy only since 1990. In Romania, which joined the EU in 2007, you can see how companies like Coca-Cola, Nestlé, Danone and South African Breweries have swallowed up local competitors. Over sixty percent of soft drinks and bottled water in Romania are now sold by Coca-Cola, the beer market is stitched up by South African Breweries and the other multinationals, and over eighty percent of food is now imported. Microsoft dominates the software market and, by investing in government lobbying, they've managed to keep Linux-based competitors, a far cheaper option, locked out. The EU backs all this up by imposing standards that only the biggest companies can afford. For example, millions of Romanian peasant farmers are no longer allowed to sell their milk outside their village, even though it's more organic than what's available in the supermarket. Another example is in Finland which, according to a friend, only has two massive milk companies – all the family farms and small dairies have been squeezed out.

But this kind of multinational-takes-over-new-market scenario is not new. We all know about it. What propels Romania into the category of World's First Dystopia is the massive cyanide mining project that could turn much of Transylvania, one of the most beautiful parts of Europe, into a wasteland. It's also a case study about how good PR and lobbying can convince a population that the destruction of their ecosystem is in their own interest. The Rosia Montana Gold Corporation, an offshore investment fund that's listed on the Toronto Stock Exchange, has promised Romanians "a thousand jobs", billions in tax dollars and – the most audacious claim that could have come straight out of *1984* – environmental protection. The reality is that three villages and four mountains will be demolished and a massive reservoir for two hundred and fourteen million tons of cyanide waste will be built (cyanide is used to extract gold from ore). Never before has such a big cyanide mining project been attempted in Europe. Rivers and groundwater in the region, including the Danube, may be poisoned and only about two hundred long-term jobs will be created – the other jobs are to do with the initial demolition process. The tax income for the nation is unknown because the company's contract with the Romanian government is a state secret, and Romania's tax laws are riddled with loopholes.

The most extraordinary thing about the Rosia Montana project is that a local residents' association has managed to block it for so long. Using volunteer lawyers they have managed to stop the project in the local courts time and again, and this shows that Romania's charity and legal sectors are not as corrupt and weak as many like to assume. The project has been a hot political issue for successive governments and most try to avoid it, while doing what they can to facilitate it on the quiet. But every Romanian government seems intimidated by the massive crowds of protesters that the project's opponents organise every time the miners make a step towards getting their operating licence. But the investors will not give up. This is a test case for the international mining industry: their business model depends on badly governed countries like Romania bending to their will and allowing unrestricted access to their mineral wealth. Defiance like this could encourage others to stand up to them, and this doesn't fit with the big mining companies' vision for our future.

## Postscript

This article was published in the Huffington Post in 2013, when massive street protests against the project were taking place in Bucharest. This was the only article I ever wrote that went viral, and I'm still proud that it was about such an important cause; in fact, someone on the street protest told me they'd seen a banner saying, *No Dystopia Here!* In the interim the evil mining company (the Rosia Montana Gold

Corporation) tried to sue the Romanian government for a staggering $3.3 billion for lost profits. The case took place in a special court in Washington DC, set up for corporations to sue governments – the technical term is an Investor State Dispute Settlement – although it didn't get anywhere. But this relentless mining company is still pushing for a licence to pollute Transylvania.

The good news is that, in 2021, UNESCO put the historic parts of the Rosia Montana village under its protection. This will make it much harder for the miners to rip up the area and pollute it with cyanide. It's a victory for local people over corporations. Finally, I got this comment from Lara, my wonderful daughter-editor: "You know *The Handmaid's Tale* was heavily influenced by Romanian women's experiences under communism? Food for thought."

# CAMBRIDGE ANALYTICA & MY ETHICAL CODE

Journalism works like this: a news story breaks and all the media channels start writing, or talking, about it. For a few days it's all over the media. Then it's forgotten. The best stories, from the media's point of view, are those which keep going for months or, in the case of wars, even years. The Cambridge Analytica story was a good one, in that it provided fodder to journalists for several months.

Outside the media organisations are thousands of freelance writers, like me, offering ideas to commissioning editors. We usually get ignored. "Go away!" is what I imagine they'd say if I got them on the phone. "We're very busy and important and you're not. Piss off. We set the news agenda and your pathetic pitch doesn't fit. Go and buy some advertising." The only way through this barrier is to offer a comment, or new insight, on a story that's currently in the news. This happened to me recently when the news of Cambridge Analytica broke. Remember them? The guys who manipulated tens of millions of Facebook accounts in the USA, helped get Trump elected, and got away with it. The news coverage mentioned a name that rang a bell and a quick check of my emails revealed the fact that Cambridge Analytica had tried to recruit me. I look back now with relief that I managed to dodge that particular bullet.

I mentioned it on Facebook, spoke to the Associated Press in Bucharest and for a day my story was all over the Romanian news. I got my fifteen minutes of fame. Then Craig Turp, who runs a think tank in Romania called Emerging Europe, asked me a simple question that resulted in the following article. He asked me what happened, and then published a shorter version of what I wrote below:

## I'm grateful to Cambridge Analytica for reminding me how important it is to have my own code of ethics

Without my ethical code I would have been sucked into all manner of corrupt opportunities that came my way in Romania, a country I worked in for seventeen years. A feature of my ethical code is to refuse work from organisations that do things I'd have to lie about. So when Mark Turnbull, one of the directors of SCL, the company that owns Cambridge Analytica, asked me to work with them on Romania's 2016 election my suspicions were immediately raised. This all took place before Cambridge Analytica made headlines for helping Trump get elected. "Who would the client be?" I asked, and "what would the work involve?"

He told me the client would be PSD, the Social Democratic Party, a controversial political party in Romania that's supported by about a third of the population. Cambridge Analytica were pitching to be PSDs election advisors and I could be part of the team. In an email dated 3rd August 2016, Turnbull described the job: "What we have offered is to embed a two-person team into the current campaign team – a political strategist and a communications specialist, but effectively with similar skill sets / roles, to provide ongoing strategic advice and assistance across the campaign (branding, copywriting, PR, media relations, digital outreach etc.) over the next 2-3 months."

I told him there was no way that I'd work for a Romanian political party. I'd spent seventeen years building up a good reputation as a problem solver, project manager, writer and PR consultant, and I didn't want to throw it all away. I also didn't want to hide the fact that an important job I'd done was unethical. I knew that working for political parties in Romania was asking for trouble as they're known to be corrupt. I didn't want to do a good job, help elect a dodgy government, and then keep it secret. Not only is transparency the best way of maintaining a good reputation but I learned, when working for a rehab clinic, that secrets themselves can be toxic. In Alcoholics Anonymous they say: You're only as sick as your secrets.

I wasn't actually living in Romania when I got this job offer. I had just moved from Bucharest to Liverpool, where I set up shop as a PR consultant. But I was struggling as my impressive foreign work experience didn't count for anything in the UK, where they don't seem to appreciate foreign work experience. Mr. Turnbull's offer was a tempting one. I urgently needed the money to pay the rent but I had a real dilemma on my hands: do I make a quick buck working for a Romanian political party, or risk eviction but maintain my reputation? I didn't take the job and I somehow managed to keep my head above water financially.

The PSD Party went on to win the Romanian elections, in December 2016, and they caused outrage by trying to undermine anti-corruption laws in order to stop investigations into their leader and wealthy supporters. Sometime later I saw Mark Turnbull on Channel Four News. Something about his face, and name, rang a bell. His colleague, Alexander Nix, was attracting a lot of media flak due to Cambridge Analytica's manipulation of social media data for Trump. Surprisingly, no criminal charges were made. Using a hidden camera, Channel Four had sent a fake prospect, an undercover journalist posing as a potential client, in a sensational sting operation. Nix was filmed stating that "we are not only the largest and most significant political consultancy in the world, but we have the most established track record. We're used to operating through different vehicles, in the shadows" and offered a "secretive relationship." Nix also talked about an undercover operation in an East European country that was so secretive that nobody even knew they were there. I realised with a shock that the country they were referring to may have been Romania, and that I could have been part of an undercover team to subvert democracy. At that moment I felt like I had dodged a bullet. My next thought was that I had to share my experience with people in Romania, so at least they would know who had been trying to manipulate them.

What's the best way to inform people in a whole country about something like this? Ironically, Facebook, where I have hundreds of personal connections with Romanians. Problem is that I only used the platform to post personal stuff and I don't usually get much feedback. Also, I was on the verge of deleting my Facebook account as an expression of disgust in their complicity with Cambridge Analytica. I ignored my disgust, swallowed my pride and posted a short description of what happened on Facebook. What came next was remarkable: I started getting feedback from some of the most interesting people I'd ever met online. It seems that a lot of people monitor my Facebook feed, which normally just consists of photos or my latest blog posts, in other words nothing particularly earth-shattering, but when something genuinely interesting comes along – they react. Several highly intelligent Romanians that I'd barely heard from until now – including journalists, political analysts and financial experts – replied with brilliant insights into the opaque world of Romanian politics, how it's financed and what foreign entities get hired to provide expertise. One of them said that he thought Cambridge Analytica didn't get the contract to provide consultancy for the 2016 election, but it went to an Israeli company. I also emailed Mark Turnbull to ask if they'd got the job on the last Romanian election and, to my surprise, he quickly replied and said they'd never worked for a Romanian political party. This doesn't mean it's not true as Cambridge Analytica themselves said on Channel Four that their role in the unnamed East European election was through a subcontractor. Liviu Dragnea, the head of PSD, Romania's ruling party, also denied the connection – and this was particularly interesting as the AP journalist who had interviewed me, and put my story on the wire, said that she'd been trying to get various statements out of this political leader for ages, but he never responded. Why did he reply to this case immediately?

Whether or not Cambridge Analytica manipulated the 2016 Romanian election isn't really the main point here. The key issue is that companies like this, which use Psychological Warfare tactics, are allowed free rein across the world to manipulate populations and enable the richest, most unethical, parties to win. It's an example of how democracy can be manipulated. Carole Cadwalladr, the Guardian journalist who first uncovered the Cambridge Analytica story, wrote "We are in the midst of a massive land grab for power by billionaires via our data. Data which is being silently amassed, harvested and stored. Whoever owns this data owns the future." As far as I'm concerned, the key point is that my personal ethical code was put to the test by this whole incident – and it worked well. It's like a firewall and it protected me from the recruitment efforts of unethical organisations, and has enabled me to avoid the wrong decisions when working in Albania, Bosnia, Tibet, and of course the UK. I imagine that being recruited by the likes of Cambridge Analytica would be like joining the mafia or an intelligence agency – you'd never be able to move on. And even if they let you go, your reputation would be besmirched and you'd be unable to find ethical work.

## Postscript

This article was written in 2018 but I didn't give much detail about my ethical code. I also have an update about the political actors in this story. This incident made me think deeply about my ethical code and I realised it was something I'd just picked up, magpie style, over the years but never actually written down. Its roots lie in ancient religions and, with this Cambridge Analytica incident, has now been tested in the Digital Age. It coped really well. Essentially, my code is just an intention to do no harm. I remember the exact moment when it started. I was in a car in Edinburgh with a redheaded woman whose name I have forgotten. She told me she had her own moral code and I remember thinking, What's a moral code? At that time I was preparing to hitchhike to Shanghai, get hired as an English teacher and stay away from Scotland for as long as possible. In order to do these things I needed to prepare psychologically and coming up with my own moral code seemed like a useful thing to do. At some point I decided to call it an ethical code as the word moral sounds rather forbidding and religious.

I was brought up a Christian and my code includes some of the ethics found within *The Bible,* such as: Do unto others as you would have them do unto you. I also spent time in Buddhist monasteries and picked up some of their philosophy too. I still remember the time in 1987 when a Buddhist monk, in a monastery in Lhasa, the capital of Tibet, told me to think about death every day. I asked him why and he said it helps you to appreciate life in general and, in particular, the present moment. I've taken useful bits from various religions but don't feel weighed down with guilt or the other negative by-products of organised religion. I respect all religions as they're based on sound morals, but don't like the way that religions get manipulated by unethical political leaders who use some of the spiritual teachings to justify policies that are, sometimes, deeply evil. I like the fact that my code was unwritten until now because if I'd written it down it would have removed the element of mystery and this is an important part of my life. Each day is a mystery to me, as is the future. I react to daily mysteries with a flexible, problem-solving approach and this works really well as it enables me to adapt easily to constant change. This is what makes me happy. It's also the way I travel: I don't study my destination before getting there, so everything is a discovery.

There is a strong element of self-interest in my ethical code and I think it's important to embrace this rather than be ashamed of it. My daughter Lara says it's proof I'm a Slytherin, as she's claimed for years. I was offended as that's where all the villains of Harry Potter are from, but Lara says that's a very pedestrian way to look at it and that I fit the traits of cunning, ambition, and resourcefulness. "You'd be great as a politician or a lobbyist," she says, "but instead your ambition is just to vibe and live like a vagrant, and by the gods do you find a way to make that work". My ethical code boils down to the principle that I try not to do things that will have a negative impact on me in the future. It's simple: don't be nasty or it will come back to bite you; but don't be weak either as bullies will always come back for more; don't work with dodgy organisations or your reputation will suffer; be honest, as lies have a nasty habit of haunting you; avoid situations where any of this is likely to happen. That's it, that's my code. I don't think an ethical code can always stop you from doing the wrong thing, but it's always there to quietly guide you in the right direction.

All this talk of ethics, morals and religion is in stark contrast to the people I've been writing about in this story. What happened to them? It's worth looking up Alexander Nix on Wikipedia as it describes a case study of privilege that has, presumably, protected him from prosecution: a wealthy landed gentry family with a mansion outside London; an Eton education; work experience in the finance sector; moving into companies that gather intelligence; meeting Boris Johnson; setting up Cambridge Analytica; getting contracts with the Conservative Party, the British Military as well as hundreds of political parties abroad.

Unlike Carol Cadwalladr, the other protagonist of this story, who suffered years of libel action, no court cases that I know of were brought against Nix. But, in 2020 he did sign a "disqualification undertaking" with the American Federal Trade Commission, agreeing not to manage any companies for the next seven years. This document is legally valid in the UK too, but it seems like a mild slap on the wrist for what he did. Part of the agreement he signed included the following text: "Within the undertaking, Alexander Nix did not dispute that he caused or permitted SCL Elections Ltd or associated companies to market themselves as offering potentially unethical services ...". The unethical services he offered included: "bribery or honey trap stings, voter dis-engagement campaigns, obtaining information to discredit political opponents and spreading information anonymously in political campaigns". I still don't understand how he got away with it.

I also have an interesting update about Liviu Dragnea, the leader of the Romanian PSD party. At the time of writing the main article above, Dragnea was a strong leader of not only the PSD party but also the Romanian government. It was a peculiar situation as Dragnea's party, the PSD, was in power at the time and although he was barred from office as he was under investigation for corruption, he ran both the party and the government with a rod of iron. It seemed high-ly unlikely that there would be any conviction against him while his party was running the country, especially consid-ering the Romanian legal system has only been independent since 1990. Part of this article describes the political corrup-tion in the USA, and how the British establishment protects their own, so surely the Romanian establishment would follow this trend and not show any courage when it comes to prosecuting high profile cases. I was amazed to hear the news in 2019 that the Romanian courts had sentenced Liviu Dragnea, who was the leader of the governing party at the time, to three and a half years of prison for political corruption. Although Dragnea had his case reduced by half, it was a stunning act of political courage and, at the time, I posted a Tweet to "All Americans," saying "Look what courage the Romanian establishment has. They've just sent their top political leader to jail. What's happening with all those legal investigations into Trump?" As with the Rosia Montana versus the cyanide mining project, Romania's legal system continues to show surprising, and remarkable, courage.

# BEAUTIFULLY WRITTEN BUT UNCONVINCING

The problem with reviewing a book is that you have to read the damn thing, which is easy enough if you're a speed reader. But I read too slowly and by the time I get to the end my enthusiasm to share has often evaporated. Often I reach a moment of revelation early on in a book and think: This is the best book I've ever read! But a friend pointed out that I tend to get over-enthusiastic about every book I'm reading. The ancient Greeks used to say that enthusiasm was a disease and, if so, then I'm a terminal case.

The book I'm writing about here is called *The Last Hundred Days* by Patrick McGuinness, and I went through the following stages with it: excitement at getting my hands on a copy (I'd heard it was good, it has rave reviews and a great cover); pleasure at reading the superb writing; and then disappointment as the story was completely out of synch with everything I know about Romania under communism. "Sinister, comic and lyrical", blares a review from The Independent on the back cover, which goes on to say: "It vividly captures the end of a long nightmare". This is true, what the book does do brilliantly is describe the crushing boredom, pointlessness and bureaucracy of life in a communist dictatorship. The London Times is quoted as saying "stunning" about the tome while the New York Times refers to it as, "observant, reflective, witty and precise".

The descriptions are beautiful, the writing superb, but when it comes to the story it falls apart as it's so unconvincing. The main character is a British guy who gets a job teaching English in Bucharest University in 1989, but he never seems to do any teaching. That in itself isn't much of a criticism, as focusing on his teaching work may not be part of the story, but it's one of the problems of credibility. The book is set in the hundred days before Romania's 1989 revolution and I was hoping the author would shed some light on an event which still has a lot of unanswered questions hanging over it, the main one being: *was the revolution planned in advance?* Many Romanians believe in conspiracy theories, in line with their ancient beliefs that they are the mere playthings of gods and emperors, and in the case of the 1989 revolution some say it was ordered by the Soviet Union and some believe the Americans were behind it. Needless to say there is no evidence for either scenario. The book offers nothing on this front, in fact there is a complete absence of political or historical insights and not even a fictional suggestion of who ordered the shooting of protesters in Timişoara, the event that sparked the uprising in Bucharest and Romania's other cities.

The Englishman's university students all speak fluent English and within a few chapters he's chatting in Romanian like a native; but not a word is written about how everyone learns each other's languages so effortlessly. When I moved to Romania in early 1990 very few people knew English, as it was barely taught in schools, and those who did had none of the fluency this author gives them. His Romanian characters speak English as if they were educated in British schools, using cultural references that not even Americans would understand. As for foreigners learning Romanian, I can think of a handful who know it fluently but I've met hundreds who have lived there for years, done endless lessons but can barely do more than order another beer. It's not so much that the Romanian language is difficult, it's similar to French and Italian, but most people aren't good at learning languages – especially the Brits and the Americans.

The plot is built around various interactions with university teachers and students, and the revolution approaches as a minor, almost irrelevant, sideshow and is barely mentioned. The main character, the Brit, comes across as a weedy intellectual yet he effortlessly seduces the best-looking girl in the class, who just happens to be the daughter of one of the most formidable men in the country – the Minister of the Interior. This would have been the man responsible for the police force, which was huge and terrifying under communism, and he could have had the English weed arrested on a whim. Anybody with any sense of self-preservation would have steered well clear of her and if the author had had more imagination he could have turned this into a comic, or dramatic, plot twist – English teacher runs off with police chief's daughter – but there's no mention of the risks involved. Maybe the author just didn't know about the dangers that meddling with such a character would involve. This reminds me of the catty saying about King James the First of England, who was also King James the Sixth of Scotland who, they say, was: *The wisest fool in Christendom.*

*The Last Hundred Days* is a novel but it breaks the main rule of good fiction: making the characters true to themselves. The author dabbles in the absurd and this is interesting as Romania under communism was absurd in many ways. This is probably a common feature in nations where one man makes almost all political decisions, resulting in expensive vanity projects and constructions that make no sense. Pre-communist Romania has a history of absurdist writers and one of the world's greatest was the Romanian born playwright Eugène Ionescu (1909-1994), who made his name in France. The Romanians have another brilliant absurdist writer – Ion Luca Caragiale (1852-1912) – whose observations on a corrupt and incompetent bureaucracy are cutting and hilarious even today. Unfortunately neither of these great wits gets a mention in this underwhelming book.

Patrick McGuinness failed to carry me off into his land of fictional make-believe, although he succeeded with the London-based book critics – none of whom, I suspect, knew the first thing about Romania. The most interesting character is the main character's teaching assistant, Leo. It's not clear if this Leo is Romanian or English as he's fluent in both cultures, as well as the languages, and he's attributed with a series of skills which are both fabulous and highly unlikely in Romania at that time. Leo's day job is to teach English at Bucharest University but nobody in authority objects to the fact that he never shows up. At his spacious apartment he has an array of photographic and video equipment and unparalleled access to the embassies and foreign media – whom he supplies with images of the ongoing demolition of Bucharest's ancient buildings. He's also writing various books about the old city.

In my experience, both teaching English and writing a book are really energy-consuming activities and, with all his video-photography-secret-filming-spy work, I would have thought that this chap would have his hands full. But no, these activities are just his hobbies – Leo's real function is to be the biggest black marketer in Bucharest. The most remarkable thing about Leo's fairy-tale existence is that he has no problem with the dreaded *Securitate,* one of the most formidable secret police forces in the former Communist Bloc. It makes for good reading and may be convincing to those who know nothing about life in communist Romania. The kind of corrupt activities that McGuinness describes certainly did go on under Ceauşescu's rule – and some say that the black market kept the people supplied with food – but it was monopolised by senior officials within the Communist Party and their illicit partners. The communists could claim that they had eliminated crime but that was only because they were monopolising it for themselves. There's no way that the secret police wouldn't have known about such a big operation as the one imagined by McGuinness, as there were said to be almost half a million informers. And if you consider that in communist Romania everyone who owned a typewriter had to take it to their local police station every year and leave a sample of its type, in case it had been used for illegal purposes, there is absolutely no chance that someone would have been allowed to operate a complete photo and video production studio, let alone roam the streets filming old buildings being knocked down.

My favourite passage in *The Last Hundred Days* describes Leo's black marketing operation: "Leo's business partner was known as 'the lieutenant': a tattooed, multiply earringed gypsy in riding britches and Cossack boots who revved his Yamaha Panther through the slums of Bucharest like an Iron Curtain Easy Rider. He wore a blue tunic with gold buttons and officer's chevrons – hence his nickname – and resembled a veteran of some Mongol rape-and-pillage squad. The Lieutenant took care of logistics. He commanded an army of Poles and romani caravaners who moved about in the night, across fields and mountains and urban wastelands, slid under razor wire and swept over electric fences, insubstantial as the dawn mist. They syphoned off petrol from the state service stations and disappeared equipment from the malfunctioning factories; they subtracted produce from the collectivised farms and re-routed flour and cooking oil from the night convoys. Inventories all over the country adjusted themselves to their passing."

There's some basis in truth in this lyrical description, but it's as "insubstantial as the dawn mist". Romania's economic system was deeply flawed, corrupt, and based on false economic reporting such as the annual harvest return that had to always be better than last year's results. The factories were only able to function because of barter arrangements with their suppliers, personal connections, bribes and desperate measures. Petty theft was rampant and known as the national sport. I believe that small scale theft by individuals was tolerated as even the secret police knew there was a hunger problem and if the crime was restricted to local areas it could be controlled, and would actually help people survive, but I can't believe the *Securitate* would have tolerated anything on a national scale – unless it was controlled by the Communist Party.

*The Last Hundred Days* reminds me of the most famous book ever to be set in Romania – *Dracula* – a book that was also written in England by a man who didn't know Romania. Bram Stoker did all his research in the British Library in London and apparently never visited the country that was, at the time, controlled by the Austro-Hungarian and Ottoman Empires. Both books have some real literary merits, but *Dracula* is a much better novel in that the characters are convincing – even the bloodthirsty count who travels around in a coffin, with earth from Transylvania, turns into a bat and lives forever.

## Postscript

Sorina Stallard, a Romanian friend who read the manuscript and gave some valuable feedback, has some objections to this article and I'm happy to share them. Sorina admits that she hasn't read the book but wants to get the audiobook version, which is strange as I'd have thought this article would put anyone off. She wrote: "The way Leo is described seems plausible and certainly part of my own experience" [of communist Romania before 1989]. "Those linked to the black market tended not to have issues with the *Securitate* whom they fed and kept in good 'spirits'. A sort of Otto in *Schindler's List*. If you wanted it to work, you had to do it in style. The bigger, the better. The smaller, the riskier."

If Sorina is right, surely such a black-market operation would have to have been a hell of a lot more discreet than in the one described in this absurd book. The word that best describes communism in Eastern Europe is grim. It can be compared to the dark, spartan, unforgiving Calvinism of my own country, Scotland, where overt displays of affection, enthusiasm or spontaneity were once frowned upon. My point is that the high priests of communist Romania would never have allowed such an outlandish operation as described in this book to exist, precisely because it had style and wasn't under the control of the communists. The centrally controlled communist nations of Eastern Europe were useless at organising the supply of industrial and farming equipment, food and every type of consumer good. Usually there was a chronic shortage, sometimes there was a glut and perhaps the main symbol of communism was the queue. The fact that they tried to centrally control everything was the problem. If they could have just allowed every factory, farmer, business and family to organise their own distribution and logistics it would have functioned much better. But the Marxist-Leninism that came to rule Romania is based on the idea that people are untrustworthy, which is an interesting contrast to the original communist ideal of the 1820s which was based on the concept that each community, or commune, should be self-governing as they are intrinsically trustworthy.

Because the communist system of supply and demand didn't work they were reliant on a black market filling the gaps and getting food to the people. The authorities were aware of it, but it also brought shame to the state as it contradicted their tenet that communism was a superior form of organisation and, of course, completely free of corruption. In my opinion, flamboyant operators like Leo would have been absorbed into the system and forced to be more discreet. Any disobedience would have been dealt with by instant imprisonment, which could be done on the flimsiest rumour.

# THE BEST TRAVEL BOOK TO TAKE TO ROMANIA

My criterion for Best Travel Book has nothing to do with travel writing, a genre that is overpopulated with preening intellectuals and macho men showing off about their adventures. My best travel book is a great book to travel with. Maybe I should call it the Best Travelling Book. My choice of book also has nothing to do with Romania but is ideal to take there. Not only is it a great travel companion, but it would be an ideal gift in a country where so many people know fluent English.

My ideal travel book is thin, lightweight and able to survive in my rucksack or bike pannier where things get crushed, soaked or smeared with oil. It must be a cheap book that I'm willing to lose and it certainly can't be a Kindle as electronic devices don't last long in these conditions. It's also a book I'd want to re-read, multiple times. For many years I had a copy of George Orwell's essays, *The Lion and the Unicorn*, stashed deep inside my bike pannier. I think Orwell is one of the best writers in the English language but none of his titles qualifies as my best travel book. I also had a copy of King Lear in my pannier but it's one of those books that I studied at school but never got around to re-reading again.

My choice of best travel book is *Utz* by Bruce Chatwin. It's a book about alchemy, emperors, Nazis, communists, secrecy, bankers, museums, madness, mystery, love and death. The story is set in mid-twentieth century Czechoslovakia, where Kaspar Joachim Utz collects porcelain figurines from the eighteenth century. He manages to preserve his unique collection in his flat in Prague, despite all the outrages committed by the Nazi and communist occupiers. As well as being addictive, this little book took me to another world and made me behave in a way that I don't do when I read books: I kept going back and re-reading bits of it, I bought copies for people, I kept looking up words and I felt a real sense of loss when I finished it. This book fitted perfectly with my nomadic lifestyle as I pick up books everywhere and, having nowhere to store them, leave them elsewhere – usually as gifts to people who I think might like them.

A history teacher once told me that if you come across a word you don't understand, your mind switches off and you'll stop reading soon after – hence the need to look up words in the dictionary. But this is a bore and I rarely do it. This amazing little book made me reach for my old *Oxford Concise Dictionary* constantly and I learned a host of new words – harlequin, cabalist, rococo, arcanum, coco-de-mer – and many more. Looking up words was no longer a pain, with Bruce Chatwin it became a delight.

*In Patagonia* by Bruce Chatwin was one of the few books that gave me the impetus to travel alone across Tibet many years ago. It was the atmosphere he conjures up that captured me, not his account of travelling across Argentina. The other books that inspired me to travel alone, for indefinite periods, were *On the Road* by Jack Kerouac, a book that describes the state of mind you need to develop in order to travel independently, and *Journey to Kars* by Philip Glazebrook – a journey to Turkey that took him across communist Europe. Glazebrook's book was one of the few titles I'd come across that even mentioned Romania, a country he criticised.

Before becoming a travel writer, Bruce Chatwin worked at Sotheby's, the renowned arts and antiques auction house in London. He worked his way up from the lowest position in the company, porter, and became one of their youngest directors ever. This is probably where he learned about the exquisite little pieces that were produced in the German town of Meissen, in the eighteenth century. *Utz* is the first book I've ever read which brings that fusty old world of antiques to life, and it works so well as he writes about the porcelain collection from Meissen, and an obsessive collector, and not the antiques business in general. He focuses on a niche within a niche. Chatwin died in January 1989, a few months before the country he had so beautifully described threw out the communists and then ceased to exist.

# ROMANIA REDUX

*This is one of the few stories I wrote specifically for this book. It was written in the Moldovan village of Vârfu Câmpului, which translates as Top of the Fields, in 2018.*

When I put this book together I had moved away from Bucharest and was living in England. I realised I must go back to Romania to check on my impressions – are they still valid? Are the people as friendly as they were, and how do they see their place in the world? But it was difficult getting away. I wasn't earning much money, I was getting complacent and Romania seemed like another lifetime away. Then Luca, my son, called from Romania. He was fifteen at the time and was spending his holiday in Bucharest, in my ex-wife's apartment. My ex-wife and my kids had moved to England in 2016 and I followed in order to be close to them. She goes back to Romania several times a year, but usually most of her time is spent sorting out problems with the apartment. Luca had lost contact with the friends he'd made at the two schools he attended in Bucharest, and was bored.

"Tata, will you come to Bucharest?"

"Eh?"

"Yeah. I want to do stuff with you in Romania."

"What sort of things?"

"Travel. I want to hitchhike with you."

"Where?"

"I dunno. I've never done it before. I want to do it but am a bit nervous. You've done it and can show me the ropes."

"Okay."

This was a welcome distraction from doing well-paid but boring consultancy work in the UK, and it felt like a real honour to be invited to travel with my son. Don't teenage kids try to get away from their parents? I must have been doing something right. I started planning a trip to Romania and soon enough I was with Luca in Bucharest. It was far too hot and I couldn't wait to hit the road. By this time we had agreed to travel by using Yes Theory, a new travel philosophy he'd found on the internet. According to Forbes magazine, "Yes Theory is a movement that encourages individuals to say 'yes' to doing things that take them out of their comfort zone in order to grow as individuals". Luca had shown me videos of young people travelling in France, asking questions to their social network followers. In one of the videos I saw the group were in Charles de Gaulle airport and they asked their followers if they should go north or south? The vote was north and so they got a ticket on the first plane north, which was to Iceland. They then asked if any of their followers were based in Iceland – Yes – and if anyone could offer accommodation and transport: Yes and Yes. A good time was had by all and an inspiring video was posted on YouTube.

It proved quite easy to implement our own version of Yes Theory. I posted a message on my Facebook page saying: "We plan to hitchhike to Transylvania and then Moldova. Do any of my Romanian friends want to meet up or offer us a bed for the night?" We got instant gratification: a Scottish guy I'd never met, who was running a farm in the Craiova region, invited us to stay with him. That was an ideal starting point for our journey as it's west of Bucharest and south of our main target of Transylvania. The next morning we were on the train to Craiova and the Scottish guy came into town to pick us up.

After an interesting evening we started hitching and, to my surprise and delight, found it to be as easy as it had been in the 1990s. By this time we had an invitation to stay with a sculptor in Târgu Jiu, a small city that has international renown for its association with Constantin Brâncuşi, the great Romanian-French sculptor. Offers of friendship kept coming and we were given free lifts across the country in cars, trucks, minibuses and even a horse and cart at one point. We camped in the Petroşani mining area, the village of Roşia Montană and on Ceahlău which was the holy mountain of the ancient Dacia people. My memory of Romanians being hospitable was still valid. We got lifts quickly, people wanted to talk, and we were offered places to stay by people who we'd only just met. Almost everyone we came into contact with was happy to share their view of the world.

I had come to Romania in a state of ignorance about their current affairs. I'd lived there for seventeen years but since moving to the UK in 2016 hadn't followed Romanian politics. But, as we travelled around in August 2018, it became impossible to avoid the news that huge protests against the government were taking place in Bucharest. Tens of thousands of progressive Romanians, including many living abroad who had come back for this purpose, were demanding the government's resignation. One of their main complaints was that the government was pushing through legislation that would undermine the struggle against corruption and lift the criminal charges against the leader of the ruling party, Liviu Dragnea. When the protests were taking place the progressives looked unstoppable. There were so many of them, they were all over the media and social networks, and it seemed like they were riding a wave of public sympathy, especially after The gendarmerie, the riot police, teargassed peaceful protesters. But I wasn't with the protesters. I was with old people in the provinces, with drivers and working class Romanians, and the overall impression I got was more nuanced than I would have expected. The people I was speaking to didn't approve of the protesters, who the government had denounced as cowards who'd run away from their motherland. But neither did they approve of the current government, and especially not the violent tactics of the gendarmes.

I started to form a picture of what the Romanians think about the protests, based on people I'd met over the course of that trip and a subsequent visit later in 2018. The main idea that was forming in my head was that the progressives in Bucharest, the protesters, with whom I personally agree, probably aren't in the majority. What I like about Romanian progressives is that they tend to have a positive outlook about Romania, as they see its potential. I think they're the vocal minority, as progressives usually are, while the bulk of the population are elderly, provincial, conservative and likely to opt for the incumbent party. I'm pretty sure the people I was meeting represent the silent majority and I think it's interesting to try and describe how they think.

If I had to use one word to sum up the typical Romanian view of life, I would say *fatalistic*. This is a word I've always known and never felt the need to look up – until now. According to the *Cambridge English Dictionary* fatalism is, "the belief that people cannot change the way events will happen and that events, especially bad ones, cannot be avoided." As far as I'm concerned this word sums up the attitude of most Romanians I've met, and also helps explain their state of mind. Ever since I first came to Romania in 1986 I've noticed that most Romanians are pessimistic. I'm a positive and optimistic person and I often find myself explaining to a Romanian why such and such idea would be good, but their bedrock of negativity leaves them feeling sceptical. For some reason that I don't understand, this has never put me off Romanians and I find that, as an optimist, I fit in well with a nation of pessimists. Maybe we complement each other?

In the 1990s, the Romanians seemed glad to have thrown off communism and assumed they would soon rejoin Europe. But there's something very wrong with the idea of rejoining a continent they're already part of. When was Romania not part of Europe? I came to understand that it's not about geography but a deeply held belief that their political system, communism, was so terrible that they felt alienated from Europe's values. It's similar to attitudes in the UK, where people talk about the continent as an entity that's separate from themselves. I used to refer to Europe in this way until a Dutch friend pointed out that Britain is very much part of Europe. Until 2007, when Romania joined the EU, there was an assumption that simply joining the European Union would result in Romania becoming as wealthy and stable as the western European countries. This shared purpose, joining the EU, became a unifying political strategy for Romania's main political parties prior to 2007. The problem was that when they did join the EU the political parties lost their strategic direction, turned on each other and seemed to focus on the grubby task of enriching themselves.

Leading up to Romania's accession to the EU in 2007, over eighty percent of the population were polled as believing in the European Union. Speaking to people about this at the time, many years ago, I realised that they hoped the EU would impose a new form of clean government on their nation. Centuries of experience had shown the Romanians that corrupt government systems had always been imposed on them by the neighbouring empires and now, finally, they were faced with a choice in the matter, the EU model, and it looked pretty good. With hindsight we can now see this was wishful thinking that was encouraged by lazy journalists and politicians who liked the look of western European nations, but couldn't be bothered to check what the EU actually is – a club of developed nations. In other words, Romania was always going to end up ruling itself within the EU. For all its sins the EU isn't an empire, it's a group of self-governing nations who trade freely among themselves and share some common rules. It's worth remembering that Romania was occupied by the Red Army in 1945 and then, more or less, controlled by the Soviet Union until 1989. One of the first things the Russians did was get the SMERSH unit of the KGB – made famous by the 1957 James Bond novel *From Russia With Love* – to set up Romania's formidable secret police structure, the *Securitate*, which had half a million informers at its peak. These terror tactics had a traumatic impact on the psychology of Romanians that can be felt even today.

Unlike Moscow, Brussels was never going to supervise Romania's government. Lara, my daughter-editor, added this comment: "it wasn't going to be a dutiful mother who explained your maths homework after work, but an absent dad who just grunted when you told him you were struggling with it". The EU system is based on a body of agreed laws, the *Acquis Communautaire*, to be implemented by the sovereign government of each member state. The EU is based on trust, that each member state will do the right thing, whereas the Soviet system was based on mistrust thus justifying Moscow's role in making all the major decisions.

The upshot of all this is that when I travelled around the country in 2018, 11 years after Romania joined the EU, the people were angry. They felt let down by the EU: where was the clean government they believed had been promised? Why was corruption as bad as it had been under the communists and the Ottomans? Why were wages so low, the cost of living so high and job security so fragile? Most people I met in 2018 were now against the EU and it was pretty obvious why: many politicians had turned from being avid supporters of the trading union into nationalistic opponents. It was an easy switch – it's much easier to blame a foreign body for your nation's ills than take responsibility for improving things. The media, always looking for sensational material, were all too happy to reproduce these messages of blame and conspiracy.

As we went round Romania and spoke to people, I could hear the voice of fatalism everywhere. One of the most common refrains is that they, the unseen powers that apparently control us all, sold off our factories after communism and now we have no industry at all. The truth is that many factories, the bankrupt ones, were indeed sold off but thousands still function. Another common complaint is that we're being manipulated – a sentiment that feeds into conspiracy theories. It's the culture of blame. Ever the optimist, I pointed out that Romania produces half of its own oil, has a big car industry and also exports ships, petrol, steel, aluminium, timber, tyres, chemicals, food, wine, tobacco, furniture, textiles, shoes, pharmaceuticals, not to mention the massive IT sector, multilingual call centres and other service industries. I am then told that these facts are irrelevant because those factories are owned by foreigners and all the profits go abroad. There is some truth in this but a lot of jobs have been created, these companies pay taxes, and unemployment has always been low in Romania. Then I'm hit with their second fatalistic salvo: this was all arranged by the global cabal that controls our lives. I've been told a hundred times that they wanted to close down Romania's industry, and farms, and turn the country into a passive market for Western goods and services – as well as a source of cheap labour. This line of thought is used to explain why Romania was accepted into the EU. It's hard to argue with these fatalistic beliefs because they're so deeply held, and encouraged by nationalist commentators on TV every evening.

It's true that Romania under Ceauşescu did build up a highly industrialised economy with factories producing almost everything you can imagine. What's impressive about this story is that it went against the Soviet economic plan for the region; apparently the Soviets had told the Romanians to specialise in agriculture and food industries, but Ceauşescu ignored this directive and somehow got away with it. In the 1980s the Romanians went through a time of great austerity as the dictator wanted to pay off the national debt. The factories became run-down and inefficient, as there was no money for maintenance or spares. One of Romania's main exports at the time was food and most was sent to the Soviet Union – resulting in terrible food shortages. Despite this, many old people look back to communism with pride at the full employment, job security, housing, constant flow of good news but they conveniently forget the lack of freedom, fear, hunger, humiliation, corruption and shortages.

Hearing all these sincerely held beliefs makes it hard for me to stand up for the economic system of my own country. How can I explain that free market liberalism has benefited Romania when so many factories have closed, so many people have emigrated and corruption has burgeoned? And how can you argue that a successful car business, Dacia, and the growth of the IT sector is a good replacement for the breadth of industry that Romania had before? It's true that western experts advised them to close down or sell off inefficient factories, many of which were propped up by vast public subsidies but getting rid of them was an essential means of balancing the budget. And Romania still has a lot of factories, but not in every small town as was the case under communism. Romania's economy seems to be in rude health and it makes steady progress, year on year, despite all the moaning and groaning of Romanian naysayers. My best argument in favour of Romania is that it's fabulously wealthy when compared to the poor nations of this world – but this point can cause offence as I am insulting them by comparing Romania to the Third World. It seems impossible to make any progress in such discussions, especially online, so I avoid them. My final question on this matter, a question I've never been able to find an answer to, is this: How would it be in the interest of the Secret Cabal That Controls The World to have Romania as a poor country? Surely the richer and more stable the nation is the more of our stuff they'd buy?

What to make of all this?

In 1989, when communism fell in Romania, the Reagan / Thatcher type of capitalism was at a high point. It was riding a wave of successful privatisations and seemed to be working. The western powers were getting rich, the EU was politically stable and when Romania opened up to the outside world this type of capitalism must have seemed like the obvious road to take. It seems incredible to look back now and think that the Romanian government, and their foreign advisors decided so easily to adopt that particular economic system – which is designed to enrich sharehold-ers. This isn't a conspiracy; it's economic policy that the main western powers govern by. Didn't anyone say, Hang on a minute! Romania has a huge industrial base. Are we sure we should advise them to break it up? What will the consequences be? On the one hand, Romania's industry was certainly a drain on public finances, as many were subsidised, and the Reagan / Thatcher approach was to burn down the old factories and move towards service industries, but on the other hand couldn't they have done more to save it? Did we offer any other economic options? Couldn't they have been encouraged to just do their own thing? A period of economic protection could have been justified, as all developed economies have protected their industries until they were ready to compete internationally. It's now clear that rapidly plunging a country into a new economic system can have dire results. One of the political problems we're facing today is that many people equate the Reagan/Thatch-er model with capitalism itself, and then throw the baby out with the bathwater. It's quite common nowadays, in my own country as well as Romania, to hear people condemning all forms of capitalism. I respond to such statements by saying something like: "The Reagan/Thatcher model is an extreme form of capitalism that's shown to benefit the rich but it's destroying the planet. Capitalism doesn't have to be like this. Government could defend small businesses instead of big ones, they could increase taxes and have more than enough to fund decent health, educational and social services. They could develop a new economic model based on renewable energy and a real attempt to reduce greenhouse gases. But they don't. Despite this I am grateful for the liberty and freedom of movement that I do have."

In the meantime I remain optimistic about Romanians as they are a good people who remain deeply moral underneath all that fatalism. As an indication of their tolerance, look at the Roma minority: the prejudice against them is virulent and it goes back centuries – the Roma were slaves in Romania for 600 years. But Romanians rarely do anything aggressive against the Roma and they generally don't condone politicians who call for violent action against this misunderstood minority.

## Postscript

This story started out as a travel piece and ended up becoming very political. I think it's an important addition to the book in that it summarises what I think about Romania politically and economically, but there are some missing elements. I want to say a few words about the gambling industry, and the Romanian Orthodox Church. Also, I now have Luca's written account of the amazing hitchhiking trip we took around Romania.

My point about gambling is this: some Romanians get furious about the exploitation going on by foreign investors, a sentiment that has some basis in reality. But most of these big companies pay taxes and are accountable. The gambling industry, which has spread like a cancer in Romania, infesting each and every town and village, is not only expert at avoiding tax but they bankrupt whole families, create gambling addicts and cause far more harm than the worst foreign investors do. I went to a conference in Bucharest about this issue and heard that the gambling industry turns over billions of euros in Romania, pays an estimated two percent of the taxes they owe, and has tens of thousands of Romanians addicted to its evil offerings. The online part of the industry is totally unregulated. It promises wealth but sucks every penny out of people who can least afford it. If you look around Bucharest today, in 2023, you'll see more banner advertising for gambling than anything else. "Out of all the EU member states," wrote Alexandru Varzaru in the investigative weekly *Kamikaze,* "our legislation is the most permissive. Romania has become a heaven for the gambling industry."

Regarding the church, I got a very interesting comment from a friend who pointed out that the church plays an important part in how Romania currently functions. He kindly read my manuscript, offered a comment on this chapter but wants to remain anonymous. I respect his opinion and know there's a lot of truth in it. My own view of religion is that the source material, the concept, the bible, is great and there are some good people who live by its ethos – especially monks and nuns. The problem is when religion and politics mix, and this is where my friend has a good point. This is what he wrote: "You've not mentioned Romania's slavish addiction to Orthodox religion, which is partly responsible for the fatalism you wrote about. I say Orthodox rather than Christian, since it's so Old Testament based. Orthodoxy is also behind the obsolete prejudice against diversity – especially homophobia but also racism. Since you were in Romania, there has been a huge influx of Asians and quite a lot of Arabs – mostly, but not only, to replace the Romanian workforce who have moved to western Europe for more money. So the prejudice, born of ignorance, against brown and black people has been worn away a little. But homophobia is still rampant, especially in rural areas. This religiosity goes hand in hand with political corruption which spreads upwards from the village halls to the government. Voters could discourage it by not accepting the bribes of hams and alcohol before local elections, and the bribes that are part of public sector contracts with private sector contractors."

Having plumbed the depths of corruption and depravity, I can now turn to something positive: my son's account of our hitching trip. In a way, he represents one part of the future of Romania in that, in 2023, he moved back to Bucharest after living in England for half of his childhood. If more young people of Romanian origin were to return to this country it could be a great thing. Despite all the gambling addiction, corrupt officials, poverty, despair and fire-breathing priests, Romania still has a lot going for it and the country is changing all the time. The following text was written by Luca in 2018, on his phone, when he was fifteen. He's unwittingly written in the stream of consciousness style, which was trendy in the 1960s – years before he was even born. I edited it with a light touch as I want to keep his voice, his style, and his tremendous energy. Here it is:

## Hitching in Transylvania, by Luca Wolfe Murray

Today we hitched from Tārgu Jiu to Petroşani in a cucumber van. We went to the abandoned Petrila mine with the intent of sneaking in and looking round. We were told that it was out of bounds and incredibly dangerous, so we decided to change plans: we went in from the back. When we got inside the mine buildings my dad, as if with no intent of survival, was using both hands to hold his phone. The massive holes in the floor were just the thing he wanted to take photos of. I kept my distance from the disaster about to happen: my dad. We eventually had lunch, sitting on a concrete step, by a massive winch that used to pull coal up from a thousand metres below.

Later we hitched to the train station, where we had left our huge rucksacks, and were ready to find a place to camp. I started talking to a man who said he'll let us use his garden: "Just 800 metres up that hill". He then introduced us to another man and said, "this is my neighbour. He'll take you to my place. I have to do something," and he went. A kilometre up the road the neighbour said something like: "follow road … turn right … a log and a river … black gate!" Then he disappeared. We both nodded but had no real idea what he had muttered in his own language.

We then followed the road and looked for a black gate. We met some people and explained ourselves but since we didn't know the guy's name, and had forgotten how he looked, they laughed as if listening to a farce. They told us about a black gate, owned by a man called Nelu, about a kilometre up the road. So, naturally, we followed these instructions and walked for three kilometres, like headless chickens, until being told by another person that "Nelu with the black gate is another kilometre up the hill." We had been as faithful to Nelu as we could but eventually gave up and asked some other people if we could camp in their yard, and so we did.

The next day we were leaving Petroșani, to get to Roșia Montana, and as soon as we stuck our thumbs out the first car stopped. It was a flashy Audi with a professional football player called Alex Neacșu behind the wheel. I fell asleep and then woke up stuck to the seat: we had reached the motorway and this guy was doing 200 kilometres an hour. Concerning was not just his speed but the fact that my dad felt the need to take a good photo of him, and the guy was looking at the camera with his thumb up. We did over 120 kilometres in less than an hour.

He dropped us off on the edge of the motorway and we soon got another lift from a guy in a rickety car. I got in the front and started talking. I mentioned how the British keep saying "stranger danger", and how my Romanian family would say: "Hitchhiking is dangerous". I turned my head to see the driver had a pistol in his hand. I burst out laughing, saying, "whoa that's so cool!" He said the gun was a replica and handed it to me. We stopped at a shop to buy 6 massive water bottles because a pipe had broken and the engine was losing water fast. We drove on and were chatting and laughing, when all of a sudden the car made some dinosaur noises, then a BANG. The car died. He pulled over, opened the bonnet to see a cloud of smoke and vapour fly out. Meanwhile my dad was just waking up in the back.

He put water in the engine but it just fired boiling water back out whilst making T-Rex noises. He told me that he was going to get a key, and that's why he was driving in the area where he picked us up. It turned out that this little trip, which broke his engine, was for the cupboard of his friend's Kürtőskalács machine.

The end.

## Note from author

Kürtőskalács, pronounced *kirt-osh-ko-latch*, is a Hungarian cake that's very popular in Romania and commonly seen on Translyvanian roadsides as well as in holiday resorts. But what is it? Wikipedia describes Kürtőskalács as "a spit cake," dating back to 1679. In other words it's a hollow cake made on a rotating wooden spit above an open flame. Wikipedia's description makes my mouth water, even though I'm a vegan: "Kürtőskalács is made from sweet, yeast dough (raised dough), of which a strip is spun and then wrapped around a truncated cone–shaped baking spit, and rolled in granulated sugar. It is roasted over charcoal while basted with melted butter, until its surface cooks to a golden-brown colour. During the baking process the sugar stuck on the kürtőskalács caramelises and forms a crisp, shiny crust. The surface of the cake can then be topped with additional ingredients such as ground walnut or powdered cinnamon."

# THANK YOU ROMANIA

A London-based journalist once told me how the British tabloid newspapers operate: "Every morning we'd have an editorial meeting and the top priority was to find a lead story that would scare people." This helped me understand how the Sun, Daily Mail and Express manage to create the sensationalism, fear, excitement, addiction to daily news – the ingredients of a highly profitable business model and the most powerful tool to influence government in the modern world. Ever since Tony Blair was Prime Minister of Britain, 1997 to 2007, British governments seem to have led the country at the whim of the tabloids. [Note from 2023: in my view, the whole Brexit debacle was the result of the tabloids hate campaign against the EU, a campaign that went on for years before the actual referendum.]

In my view, the British tabloids should thank Romania for providing it with so much great material over the last quarter century. When I wrote this article in 2013 one of the headlines, written in response to an EU freedom of move-ment directive, was: "27 million Romanian and Bulgarian scroungers are coming over in January 2014." That was just one example of the endless waves of distorted scare stories that have been printed about immigrants in the UK. The implications of that headline are that the entire population of both these countries were about to come to Britain, and the irony is that Britain has become one of the least popular destinations for citizens of Romania and Bulgaria as these insulting news stories get reproduced in their own media.

Another great tabloid news story that emerged from Romania was Nicolae Ceaușescu, the communist dictator who was overthrown by a mob in 1989. It was the first televised revolution and the media loved every minute of it. But the triumph in ousting one of the region's worst tyrants was short lived – it was soon overtaken by stories about the state of children in the network of run-down children's homes. These grim institutions were called orphanages by the media, even though almost all of the kids held captive had living parents. What the British rags didn't say is that Romania had opened its children's homes to international assistance, unlike their neighbouring countries which strictly banned outsiders from visiting such institutions. What this transparency meant was that foreign journalists could flood in and make them look like hell. This wasn't a conspiracy designed to make Romania look bad, it was just that international journalists, including myself, had no idea that the situation was just as bad in neighbouring countries. We lacked context and were ignorant about the region we were now writing about.

It was ironic that of all the countries of Central and Eastern Europe, Romania was the one that implemented the most comprehensive child welfare reform process – a good news story the British media predictably ignored. Thanks to one of the most successful EU-reform programmes in the region, child welfare in Romania has been totally reformed: it's now illegal to institutionalise children under the age of two; all abandoned children now go directly to foster families; and it's one of the few poor countries anywhere in the world that has successfully banned the sale of children under the dubious label of international adoption. Some years ago I worked as a PR expert for an EU-funded project which raised awareness about Romania's successful legislation on children's rights. My job was to tell international journalists that things had changed, that babies were no longer being institutionalised, or sold abroad, and that foster care was the order of the day. There were still huge problems due to poverty and corruption, but a fundamental change had been made. The American, Dutch, Russian and French media were open to this news but British editors were unwilling to let their journalists come and investigate. Eventually I found out why: I got through on the phone to a British tabloid editor who told me: "Whenever we need a horror story about institutionalised children we send someone to Romania, where they can always find a sad case to report on. These stories don't have the same appeal when they come from Bulgaria, the Czech Republic or Russia – even though the situation there may be just as bad." He seemed interested that Romania was the only Central and Eastern European country to have reformed its child welfare system but said, "This isn't a news story. You must know the old adage: 'Good news is no news'. News editors like to assign particular stories to specific countries so that readers will make immediate associations."

Partly due to the toxicity of the media, but also because of Romania's inability to do good PR, the Romania label used by the British tabloids continues to be: orphan, gypsy, beggar, thief, welfare-scrounger. To explain that there are so many Roma people in Romania because they weren't wiped out in the Second World War, as happened in some of the neighbouring countries, or that most Romanians have no intention of moving to the UK, or that the vast majority of Romanians are hard-working and honest, is too complicated and boring for British newspaper editors. It's much easier to base their reporting on generalisations and barely concealed prejudice. In my view, the British tabloid media should issue a public thank you to Romania for providing it with so much sensational material over the years. Another group that should send a thank you message to Romania are businesses all over Europe. Countless European companies have benefited by hiring reliable and grateful Romanian workers, and many have profited since this nation of almost twenty million consumers was opened to the free market. It's one of the biggest new markets in this part of the world and western companies have, since the fall of communism, flooded it with imports.

Everyone I know in the UK who has worked with a Romanian, or hired one to fix up their home, have been delighted with their uncomplaining attitude, skill, hard work and, in the case of recently arrived and hungry-for-work tradesmen, low cost. Many people assume that all Romanians who come to Britain are unqualified workers. This is not the case. Every type of skilled and unskilled worker comes over, as well as artists and professionals of every type. The first Romanian I met in Britain was in the 1970s, when I was a kid in Edinburgh: an artist called Paul Neagu (1938–2004). The Tate Gallery's website describes him as: "a Romanian artist who worked in diverse media such as drawing, sculpture, performance art and watercolour .... His influences included Cubism, Marcel Duchamp, Constantin Brancusi, Joseph Beuys. His works can be found in public collections ...".

In 1987, two years before the fall of communism, I met an architect who now has a flourishing architecture business in Scotland. His late wife was an artist specialising in delicate and unique porcelain sculptures. His current wife, also a Romanian, is a Scottish-qualified judge who works as a legal expert for Glasgow City Council. Since the revolution I have met, in the UK, Romanian filmmakers, a puppeteer, a telephone engineer, a DJ (Nico de Transilvania), a City broker, a poetess, several business owners, a maths teacher, a sociologist, entrepreneurs, a famous violinist (Alex Bălănescu) and a not so famous violinist (Monica Lucia Madas), a cellist, teacher, university lecturer, photographer, IT experts; and a doctor, nurse, driver and administrator at the Scottish rehab clinic where I used to work.

The one person who did thank Romania was a TV celebrity who's famous for being boorish, politically incorrect and inconsiderate: Jeremy Clarkson. I've heard this highly successful cynic warn people to avoid some of the most popular countries on earth – such as Italy and the USA – so I was really surprised to hear him praise a country that some love to hate. At the end of a Top Gear programme about Romania in which he described the Trans-Făgărașan mountain pass as "the best road in the world", he thanked Romania "for having us," and then said he'd like to come back "forever". Normally the only words of praise coming from this man's mouth are sarcastic, but in this case they seemed genuine. Clarkson is just one of the many Brits, myself included, who fell in love with this beautiful but under-appreciated nation.

## Postscript

There are two things missing from this article: a thank you to Romania from me and more details about international adoption, an issue I briefly mentioned above. I can resolve the first thing easily by simply writing the words Thank You Romania: You have been the making of me! The second issue, international adoption, is more complicated but it's also very current. On the 17th of March 2023 the International Criminal Court in the Hague issued an arrest warrant for Vladimir Putin, president of the Russian Federation, for being "allegedly responsible for the war crime of unlawful deportation of population (children) and that of unlawful transfer of population (children) from occupied areas of Ukraine to the Russian Federation." In other words, the Russians have been kidnapping Ukrainian children and putting them up for adoption in Russia. As shocking as this seems, it's actually quite common: the Americans made it into an international business model in South Korea and Vietnam; when thousands of children, declared abandoned by the private adoption agencies, were "saved". The fact that most of these children were simply homeless because of the war, and had extended families who would have been willing to take them in, was ignored at the time and is only coming out now, a generation later.

I wrote a lot about international adoptions, and don't want to get into it too deeply here. But I would like to quote from this opinion article I wrote in the EU Observer in 2009. It was published under the title, Romania Should Withstand Pressure to Lift Ban on International Adoptions:

Ever since Romania prohibited international adoptions in 2001 it has been pressured by the leaders of France, Italy, Israel, Spain and the USA to lift the ban. Behind these politicians are private adoption agencies, adoptive parents and others interested in getting children. When Hillary Clinton, US Secretary of State, met the Romanian Foreign Minister earlier this year she handed him a letter which included the statement: "We urge you to reform current law in Romania … including a reevaluation of your decision to remove international adoption as an important permanency option".

Romania should continue to stand firm in the face of this intense lobby for international adoption, a lobby which talks about tens of thousands of Romanian orphans languishing in grim institutions. But the EU-funded reform of Romania's child welfare system resulted in the closure of almost all the notorious children's homes, introduced foster care and a range of family-based alternatives. The EU also insisted that Romania stop international adoptions as it had established a free market in children [as a condition for its accession into the EU].

The truth is that there are very few orphaned children in Romania, where abandoned children are placed in the extended family, foster or family type homes. In addition, there is a waiting list of Romanian families who want to adopt – the problem is they don't pay and therefore the incentive is to sell the children abroad. The Romanian adoption system developed in 1997, in compliance with the Hague Adoption Convention, showed that the financial incentives involved in international adoptions, up to 30,000 euro a child, corrupted health, welfare and legal services and poor single mothers were routinely persuaded to abandon their children in maternity hospitals. In other words, the demand for children created the supply which corrupted legal and social services ....

The point of mentioning international adoption in this final chapter is to show another feather in Romania's cap. Despite all the problems I've highlighted in this book, there are three successes that stand above all the failures: Romania's courage in standing up to the powerful lobby for international adoption; putting the top political leader of the country in jail, while his party was still in office; and standing up to the massive offshore fund that wants to build a massive cyanide lake in the Transylvanian village of Roșia Montana. All three of these decisions show great courage on the part of the Romanian political and legal system. For all the bad news that people say about Romania, for all the doom and gloom, these three facts are a constant reminder that this nation has spine and guts. Also, while we're on the subject of Romania's achievements, the country keeps making small steps towards economic prosperity. At the time of writing this concluding statement, in March 2023, I looked at the website of the IMF (International Monetary Fund) to see how Romania's GDP growth compared to my own country, the UK. The results were grim, but not for the reason you might assume: Romania's GDP growth is recorded at three point one percent which is quite healthy, while the UK's is predicted to actually shrink. The IMF says the UK's growth is estimated to be negative zero point six percent. This isn't the sort of fact that would make it into a newspaper report, but this level of steady economic growth has been quietly happening for most of the last twenty years in Romania and my own view is that the country is gradually building herself up economically. If this kind of progress continues, and the political situation doesn't fall apart, Romania will be in a much better place in the not too distant future.

# AFTERWORD

I like to tell people that I live in a park as it creates the
impression that I'm a tramp. I don't know why but I find
this funny. Maybe I have an infantile sense of humour. After
seeing the shock and confusion in my interlocutor's face,
I then tell the rest of my story: I actually live on a houseboat called Marge the Barge which is moored in the middle
of Reading. I'm five minutes from Reading Station and a
further thirty minutes, on a train, will get me to Paddington
and the fleshpots of London. On one side of my wheel-
house-writing-den is the River Thames and on the other is
the park, which is called Christchurch Meadows.

I love living on a houseboat. It suits me in so many
ways. I don't mind emptying my own sewage as it makes
me aware of my impact on the planet and, incidentally,
this is the aspect of houseboat life that some people find
most interesting. I love the transient nature of our mooring
– maybe we'll get kicked out of this city-centre park and
have to move to a remote bit of countryside. I love the idea
that you can move house by just turning on the engine and
heading along the river. I love the community, and I don't
mean other houseboat folk, I mean the constant action going
on between the birds. There are so many birds around that I
feel like I am part of their community.

The Canada Geese are the thugs of the park and they
strut along the pathways, crapping everywhere, hissing at
people and only giving ground when a psychotic lapdog
goes for them. The geese seem to be constantly fighting
passers-by, dogs, or each other. They are creatures of war
and don't seem to know fear. One day I saw a gaggle of
geese waddling through the park, in a straight line, as if they
were policemen looking for evidence after a crime. There
was something militaristic about their stiff movements and

aggressive barks. What came next reminded me of reading about ancient battles, when soldiers would move in huge formations: a brown spaniel came into the park and ran towards them at full pelt. At first the geese didn't react but then, in one movement, the whole flock was airborne. The dog was racing around trying to get his teeth into something, but the geese were flying away and honking their outrage at the incursion.

The swans are less aggressive than the geese, but always ready to inspect whatever it is I might be throwing into the river, usually just coffee grinds. What I love about swans is the way they take off and land. They need about a hundred metres to get airborne and they use their huge, flat feet making a curious flapping sound as they run along the top of the water, gaining the momentum to take off. When they land they use their feet like the floats on seaplanes, briefly surfing before settling down in the water. Swans also spend a lot of time with their bums in the air, using their long necks to grub around in the slime on the riverbed. Ducks are everywhere and I admire them for not being intimidated by their much bigger cousins. They also look fabulous and have richer colours than anything else on the river. The ducks hang around the fringes, always ready to nip in and grab a bit of sliced white bread that granny and the kids have thrown into the river. They move faster than the other water birds. Seagulls only make an occasional appearance on the river and I'm not sure why this is, as they tend to dominate urban spaces. Maybe they're too busy patrolling Reading city centre, where there are plenty of rich pickings left by the hordes of commuters who pass by every day.

What's all this got to do with my stories from Romania?

The reason I put this book together is because one of the people I shared the houseboat with – Jyoti Pancholi – told me she was going to Romania and wanted to know what I thought of her proposed itinerary. I told her that I think it's a great route as getting around Romania is slow, as the roads are terrible and the trains are decrepit. But the route she'd chosen was good as her choice of locations, Deva, Braşov and Bucharest, are all accessible by train. I offered to email her some of the stories I'd published about Romania over the years as some of them might be of interest.

"Do you think you'd be able to get that to us before we go?" She asked.

"Sure," I replied, "I can send them to you now".

Then it struck me: I'll collect up all the stuff I've written about Romania and put them in a volume! That was the moment when the idea for this book was born.

"I can do it in ten minutes," I said.

"That would be cool."

Did I detect a note of scepticism in her voice? Was she thinking: "Yeah, right …. Like he's going to produce a book for us, in the next month!"

But it took six months to pull this little collection of stories together. Initially, I had blithely assumed that all that was required was a bit of copy / paste, but soon realised that many of my stories were out of date, annoying, repetitive or just crap. Most of them never made the grade and aren't included here. Making the selection took ages; it was particularly difficult to get the running order right; to ensure there was a good flow between themes. I kept chopping and changing. Some of the old stuff was good but it all needed editing. In order to fill gaps in the portrait of Romania I was making, I wrote several new articles. Then I sent the manuscript to some friends, got plenty of useful feedback, incorporated it and thought I was ready. But I hadn't reckoned with my fiercely intelligent daughter Lara, who was the last one to see the manuscript. She sent me a detailed critique on almost every page and I realised I didn't have time to re-do the whole thing. Four years passed and it's only now, in March of 2023, when I happened to be in Romania for a month, that I found the time to finish it. And it wouldn't have happened had a friend, Sönke Martin, not let me use his empty apartment in Bucharest.

Since you're here I assume you don't object if I ramble on about travel writing. I sometimes describe myself as a travel writer, but when I do this I cringe inside as the ironic truth is that I don't like most travel writing: Most of it seems to be written by clever dicks or macho men who make me feel I could never do what they're doing. My first travel book was called *9 Months in Tibet,* and when I showed it to a literary agent in Scotland she said: "It's not literary enough!" I wanted to say, Neither is ninety nine percent of the population! If you want to see the dark side of travel writing you only have to look at the so-called quality British newspapers like *The Times, Telegraph and Guardian.* The travel sections of these rags have been taken over by the wealthy travel industry. Most of the articles you see there have been paid for by resorts, hotels or travel companies, and I can feel the conflict in the journalist. He wants to say the place is boring, and the country is corrupt, but he knows he mustn't bite the hand that feeds him. I spoke to a journalist at the *Daily Telegraph* recently and he told me the travel sections are cash cows for the paper – in other words those pages generate a lot of money for the newspaper.

A final word about Romanians. I've said they're really friendly but this can be deceptive. They can come across as quite hostile when you first encounter them in a shop, restaurant or bus. But when they realise you're not a Romanian this hostility tends to melt away and soon enough their friendly character comes out. My conclusion is that Romanians don't like Romanians – they seem to despise their governments, they don't trust each other, and I'm sure this is a legacy of communism. But they like foreigners and especially the Brits and Americans, which is something I've never really understood. I have travelled all over eastern

Europe and my impression is that the Slavic people of Bulgaria, Poland and the former Yugoslavia are more polite and efficient than the Romanians. They are more superficially friendly, but there seems to be an emotional wall behind that first impression. In my experience there's not much warmth or real friendliness behind that politeness (I would apply the same criticism to parts of southern England). In Romania, which is a Latin country with similarities to Italy, you can usually get to their friendly character quite easily – you just have to put up with a bit of superficial hostility.

I first went to Romania in 1986 and really hated it. The country was still under a communist dictatorship and people were too afraid to speak to me, or even to look at me. They looked depressed and grey and the lack of streetlights made it look spooky at night. Four days felt like a month. But when I went back in 1990 they were eager to engage with outsiders and I felt welcome. I lived in Romania, off and on, for seventeen years and felt completely at home there. I would love to get a traditional cottage in the mountains and retire amongst friendly villagers, but I know this is a fantasy as the forces of globalisation have destroyed the villages far more efficiently than communism did. I'll probably just become another foreigner who loves Romania and visits every few years – not such a bad compromise.

Do get in contact if you have any feedback about this book, or any questions about Romania, even though I'm currently based in the UK and don't try to keep up with its chaotic politics. I'm still a backpacker at heart, always on the move and have no idea where I'll be when you read this. You can find me on Instagram or old-fashioned email: wolfemurray@gmail.com.

Finally, you might be interested in some of my other books, all of which are available on Amazon:

*Himalayan Bus Plunge & Other Stories from Nepal* is a collection of stories and observations that's quite similar to the book you've just finished reading.

*9 Months in Tibet* is considered funny and "unput-downable", to quote a professor of Tibetan Studies at the Sorbonne. I sent the manuscript to Alexander McCall Smith and, to my delight, he wrote me a foreword.

*The Wind and the Castle* is a fairy tale that was inspired by my divorce and Hermann Hesse's fairy tales. People ask me if it's for kids and I say, "it's for everyone".

That's it from me.
Bucharest, Romania, 2023

# STARGAZING
# 2011

MONTH-BY-MONTH GUIDE TO THE NORTHERN NIGHT SKY

## HEATHER COUPER & NIGEL HENBEST

www.philips-maps.co.uk

HEATHER COUPER and NIGEL HENBEST are internationally recognized writers and broadcasters on
astronomy, space and science. They have written more
than 30 books and over 1000 articles, and are the
founders of an independent TV production company
specializing in factual and scientific programming.

Heather is a past President of both the British
Astronomical Association and the Society for Popular
Astronomy. She is a Fellow of the Royal Astronomical
Society, a Fellow of the Institute of Physics and a former
Millennium Commissioner, for which she was awarded
the CBE in 2007. Nigel has been Astronomy Consultant
to *New Scientist* magazine, Editor of the *Journal of the
British Astronomical Association* and Media Consultant to
the Royal Greenwich Observatory.

Published in Great Britain in 2010
by Philip's,
a division of Octopus Publishing Group Limited
(www.octopusbooks.co.uk)
Endeavour House, 189 Shaftesbury Avenue,
London WC2H 8JY
An Hachette UK Company (www.hachette.co.uk)

**TEXT**
Heather Couper and Nigel Henbest (pages 6–53)
Robin Scagell (pages 61–64)
Philip's (pages 1–5, 54–60)

ISBN 978–1–84907–117–8

Printed in China

*Title page: Veil Nebula (Peter Shah/Galaxy)*

## ACKNOWLEDGEMENTS

All star maps by Wil Tirion/Philip's, with extra
annotation by Philip's.
Artworks © Philip's.

**All photographs courtesy of
Galaxy Picture Library:**
Bob Purbrick *36*;
Eddie Guscott *16, 20, 28*;
Ian King *44*;
Thierry Legault *64 top right*;
Optical Vision Ltd *64 top left*;
Philip Perkins *33*;
Robin Scagell *12, 24, 61, 62, 64 bottom right*;
Peter Shah *8, 40, 48, 53, 63*.

# CONTENTS

The sight of diamond-bright stars sparkling against a sky of black velvet is one of life's most glorious experiences. No wonder stargazing is so popular. Learning your way around the night sky requires nothing more than patience, a reasonably clear sky and the 12 star charts included in this book.

*Stargazing 2011* is a guide to the sky for every month of the year. Complete beginners will use it as an essential night-time companion, while seasoned amateur astronomers will find the updates invaluable.

## THE MONTHLY CHARTS

Each pair of monthly charts shows the views of the heavens looking north and south. They are usable throughout most of Europe – between 40 and 60 degrees north. Only the brightest stars are shown (otherwise we would have had to put 3000 stars on each chart, instead of about 200). This means that we plot stars down to 3rd magnitude, with a few 4th-magnitude stars to complete distinctive patterns. We also show the ecliptic, which is the apparent path of the Sun in the sky.

## USING THE STAR CHARTS

To use the charts, begin by locating the north Pole Star – Polaris – by using the stars of the Plough (see May). When you are looking at Polaris you are facing north, with west on your left and east on your right. (West and east are reversed on star charts because they show the view looking up into the sky instead of down towards the ground.) The left-hand chart then shows the view you have to the north. Most of the stars you see will be circumpolar, which means that they are visible all year. The other stars rise in the east and set in the west.

Now turn and face the opposite direction, south. This is the view that changes most during the course of the year. Leo, with its prominent 'sickle' formation, is high in the spring skies. Summer is dominated by the bright trio of Vega, Deneb and Altair. Autumn's familiar marker is the Square of Pegasus, while the winter sky is ruled over by the stars of Orion.

The charts show the sky as it appears in the late evening for each month: the exact times are noted in the caption with the chart. If you are observing in the early morning, you will find that the view is different. As a rule of thumb, if you are observing two hours later than the time suggested in the caption, then the following month's map will more accurately represent the stars on view. So, if you wish to observe at midnight in the middle of February, two hours later than the time suggested in the caption, then the stars will appear as they are on March's chart. When using a chart for the 'wrong' month, however, bear in mind that the planets and Moon will not be shown in their correct positions.

## THE MOON, PLANETS AND SPECIAL EVENTS

In addition to the stars visible each month, the charts show the positions of any planets on view in the late evening. Other planets may also be visible that month, but they will not be on the chart if they have already set, or if they do not rise until early morning. Their positions are described in the text, so that you can find them if you are observing at other times.

We have also plotted the path of the Moon. Its position is marked at three-day intervals. The dates when it reaches First Quarter, Full Moon, Last Quarter and New Moon are given in the text. If there is a meteor shower in the month, we mark the position from which the meteors appear to emanate – the *radiant*. More information on observing the planets and other Solar System objects is given on pages 54–57.

Once you have identified the constellations and found the planets, you will want to know more about what's on view. Each month, we explain one object, such as a particularly interesting star or galaxy, in detail. We have also chosen a spectacular image for each month and described how it was captured. All of these pictures were taken by amateurs. We list details and dates of special events, such as meteor showers or eclipses, and give observing tips. Finally, each month we pick a topic related to what's on view, ranging from the Milky Way to double stars and space missions, and discuss it in more detail. Where possible, all relevant objects are highlighted on the maps.

## FURTHER INFORMATION

The year's star charts form the heart of the book, providing material for many enjoyable observing sessions. For background information turn to pages 54–57, where diagrams help to explain, among other things, the movement of the planets and why we see eclipses.

Although there is plenty to see with the naked eye, many observers use binoculars or telescopes, and some choose to record their observations using cameras, CCDs or webcams. For a round-up of what's new in observing technology, go to pages 61–64, where equipment expert Robin Scagell shares his knowledge.

If you have already invested in binoculars or a telescope, then you can explore the deep sky – nebulae (starbirth sites), star clusters and galaxies. On pages 58–60 we list recommended deep-sky objects, constellation by constellation. Use the appropriate month's maps to see which constellations are on view, and then choose your targets. The table of 'limiting magnitude' (page 58) will help you to decide if a particular object is visible with your equipment.

Happy stargazing!

Early-risers this month will be treated to the sight of a dazzling Morning Star – the planet Venus. Those of us with a more nocturnal disposition will have to wait until December, when our neighbour-world reappears in the evening sky.

Plus – we'll have a partial eclipse of the Sun at sunrise on 4 January.

But the glory of the heavens this month belongs to the stars. **Orion**, **Taurus**, **Gemini** and **Canis Major** make up a scintillating celestial tableau, and there's no better time to start finding your way around the sky.

### JANUARY'S CONSTELLATION

Crowned by **Sirius**, the brightest star in the sky, **Canis Major** is the larger of **Orion**'s two hunting dogs. He is represented as chasing **Lepus** (the Hare), a very faint constellation below Orion, but his main target is Orion's chief quarry, **Taurus** (the Bull) – take a line from Sirius through Orion's belt, and you'll spot the celestial bovine on the other side. Arabian astronomers accorded great importance to Canis Major, while the Indians regarded both cosmic dogs (**Canis Minor** lies to the left of Orion) as being 'watch-dogs of the Milky Way' – which runs between the two constellations.

To the right of Sirius is the star **Mirzam**. Its Arabic name means 'the Announcer,' because the presence of Mirzam heralded the appearance of Sirius, one of the most venerated stars in the sky. Just below Sirius is a beautiful star cluster, **M41**. This loose agglomeration of over a hundred young stars – 2500 light years away – is easily visible through binoculars, and even to the unaided eye. It's rumoured that the Greek philosopher Aristotle, in 325 BC, called it 'a cloudy spot' – the earliest description of a deep-sky object.

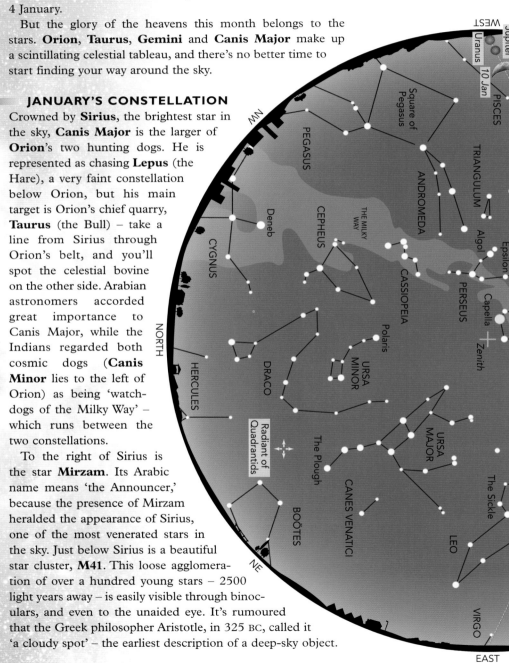

▼ The sky at 10 pm in mid-January, with Moon positions at three-day intervals either side of Full Moon. The star positions are also correct for 11 pm at *the beginning of January, and 9 pm at the end of the month. The planets move slightly relative to the stars during the month.*

## PLANETS ON VIEW

The year begins with the two brilliant planets at opposite ends of the night: Jupiter lording it over the evening sky, and Venus lighting up the dawn.

Giant planet **Jupiter** lies in Pisces: at magnitude −2.2 it far outshines any of the constellation's dim stars. At the start of January, Jupiter sets at 11 pm, but it slips below the horizon by 9.30 pm at the end of the month.

The first few days of January are also the ideal time for getting to know **Uranus**, which lies just half a degree to the upper right of Jupiter. Theoretically visible to the naked eye, binoculars will easily show you the seventh planet: at magnitude +5.9, Uranus is roughly the same brightness as Jupiter's moons.

With a telescope, you can catch **Neptune**, the most distant planet, at the beginning of January (when it sets at 8 pm), but by the end of the month it has sunk into the twilight. At magnitude +7.9, Neptune lies in Capricornus.

**Saturn**, shining at magnitude +1.0 in Virgo, rises at 0.40 am at the beginning of January, and by 10.45 pm at the end of the month.

For early birds, the dawn skies are the domain of brilliant **Venus**, which is at greatest elongation west on 8 January. At magnitude −4.3, the Morning Star may be bright enough to cast shadows! At the start of 2011, Venus rises at 4 am, slipping to 4.45 am by the end of January. Through a small telescope, you'll see the cloudy planet half-lit by the Sun.

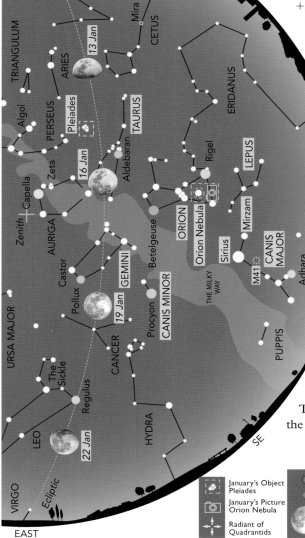

| | MOON | | |
|---|---|---|---|
| **Date** | **Time** | **Phase** | |
| 4 | 9.03 am | New Moon | |
| 12 | 11.31 am | First Quarter | |
| 19 | 9.21 pm | Full Moon | |
| 26 | 12.57 pm | Last Quarter | |

During the first couple of weeks of January, you may also catch the innermost planet, **Mercury**, loitering very low in the south-east before dawn. At its greatest western elongation, on 9 January, Mercury shines at magnitude −0.2, some 40 times fainter than Venus.

**Mars** is too close to the Sun to be seen this month.

## MOON

The crescent Moon lies near Jupiter on the evenings of 9 and 10 January. On 15 January, the Moon is near the Pleiades (Seven Sisters), and it passes Saturn on the night of 24/25 January. In the early morning of 29 January, the crescent Moon forms a striking pair with Venus, with red giant Antares to its right; the following morning, the Moon lies directly under the Morning Star.

## SPECIAL EVENTS

On **3 January**, the Earth is at perihelion, its closest point to the Sun.

The maximum of the **Quadrantid** meteor shower occurs on the night of **3/4 January**. These shooting stars are tiny particles of dust shed by the old comet 2003 EH$_1$, burning up as they enter the Earth's atmosphere. This is an excellent year for observing the Quadrantids, as moonlight won't interfere.

On the morning of **4 January**, we're treated to an eclipse of the Sun. It's not total anywhere in the world, but people in the south-east of the UK will see a great partial eclipse – provided you've got a good view of sunrise!

The Sun is 70% eclipsed by the Moon when it pops above the horizon at 8.10 am. The Moon moves steadily away, until the eclipse ends at 9.30 am. Don't expect to see the Sun's outer atmosphere, the corona, or its flaming chromosphere – these are only visible during a total eclipse. Instead, the Sun will look as if it has had a chunk taken out of it.

**DO NOT LOOK AT THE SUN DIRECTLY: PROJECT ITS IMAGE USING A PINHOLE, OR USE SPECIAL ECLIPSE GOGGLES.**

## JANUARY'S OBJECT

The **Pleiades** star cluster is one of the most familiar sky-sights. Though it's well known as the Seven Sisters, most people see any number of stars but seven! Nearly everyone can pick out the six brightest stars, while very keen-sighted observers can discern up to 11 stars. These are just the most luminous in a group of 500 stars, lying about 400 light years away (although there's an ongoing debate about the precise distance!). The brightest stars in the Pleiades are hot and blue, and all the stars are young – less than 80 million years old. They were born together, and have yet to go their separate ways. The fledgling stars have blundered into a cloud of gas in space, which looks like gossamer on webcam images. Even to the unaided eye or through binoculars, they are still a beautiful sight.

## JANUARY'S PICTURE

The great **Orion Nebula** is lit by fierce radiation from a small cluster of newly-born stars called 'the Trapezium'. It's part of a huge gas complex, which has enough material to create half a million baby suns.

## JANUARY'S TOPIC
### Constellations

**Canis Major,** our constellation of the month, highlights humankind's obsession to 'join up the dots' in the sky, and weave stories around them – even if the shape of the star pattern bears little relation to its name.

◄ *The Orion Nebula, photographed by Peter Shah using a 200 mm Newtonian reflector from Meifod, Powys. He gave 30-minute exposures through red, green and blue filters for the main nebula, plus separate 1-minute exposures in each colour for the central area, which would otherwise be overexposed.*

But why? One answer is that the constellations on view change during the year as the Earth moves around the Sun, and the constellations acted as an '*aide memoire*' to where we are in our annual cycle – something of particular use to the ancient farming communities.

Another is that the stars were a great steer to navigation at sea. In fact, scholars believe that the Greek astronomers 'mapped' their legends on to the sky specifically so that sailors crossing the Mediterranean would associate certain constellations essential to navigation with their traditional stories.

But not all the world saw the sky through western eyes. The Chinese divided up the sky into a plethora of tiny constellations – with only three or four stars apiece. And the Australian Aborigines, in their pitch-black deserts, were so overwhelmed with stars that they made constellations out of the dark places where they couldn't see any stars!

The winter star-patterns are starting to drift towards the west, setting earlier – a sure sign that spring is on the way. The constantly changing pageant of constellations in the sky is proof that we live on a cosmic merry-go-round, orbiting the Sun. Imagine it: you're in the fairground, circling the Mighty Wurlitzer on your horse, and looking out around you. At times you spot the ghost train; sometimes you see the roller-coaster; and then you swing past the candy-floss stall. So it is with the sky – and the constellations – as we circle our local star. That's why we get to see different stars in different seasons.

## FEBRUARY'S CONSTELLATION

Spectacular **Orion** is one of the rare star groupings that looks like its namesake – a giant of a man with a sword below his belt, wielding a club above his head. Orion is fabled in mythology as the ultimate hunter.

The constellation contains one-tenth of the brightest stars in the sky: its seven main stars all lie in the 'top 70' of brilliant stars. Despite its distinctive shape, most of these stars are not closely associated with each other – they simply line up, one behind the other.

Closest is the star that forms the hunter's right shoulder, **Bellatrix**, at 240 light years. Next is blood-red **Betelgeuse** at the top left of Orion, 600 light years away.

The constellation's brightest star, blue-white **Rigel**, is a vigorous young star more than twice as hot as our Sun, and 50,000 times as bright. Rigel lies 800 light years from us, roughly the same distance as the star that marks the other corner of Orion's tunic – **Saiph** – and the two outer stars of the belt, **Alnitak** (left) and **Mintaka** (right).

We must travel 1300 light years from home to reach the middle star of the belt, **Alnilam**. And at the same distance, we

▼ *The sky at 10 pm in mid-February, with Moon positions at three-day intervals either side of Full Moon. The star positions are also correct for 11 pm at the beginning of February, and 9 pm at the end of the month. The planets move slightly relative to the stars during the month.*

find the stars of the 'sword' hanging below the belt – the lair of the great **Orion Nebula** (see Object and January's Picture).

## PLANETS ON VIEW

Vying for attention with the giant of the constellations, Orion, we have the giant of the planets, **Jupiter**, putting on its last good evening show this year. Brilliant in the western sky at magnitude −2.0, in the dim constellation of Pisces, Jupiter sets at 9.25 pm at the start of February – but by the end of the month it's setting as early as 8.00 pm. Grab a pair of binoculars, and view the ever-changing pattern of the planet's four biggest moons as they orbit Jupiter, sometimes passing behind or in front of the celestial giant.

**Uranus** also lies in Pisces, glowing on the borderline of naked-eye visibility at magnitude +5.9. It's setting at 7.45 pm at the beginning of the month, but the planet sinks into invisibility in the twilight glow by the end of February.

Ringworld **Saturn**, at magnitude + 0.9, is rising at 10.40 pm when the month opens, and by 8.45 pm at the end of February. You'll find it in the constellation Virgo.

Last, but certainly not least, in the planetary parade is **Venus**, a celestial beacon at magnitude −4.1 in the south-eastern skies before dawn. The Morning Star is rising at 4.50 am at the start of February, but it's gradually dropping towards the Sun and rises at 5.10 am by month's end. Through a telescope, you'll see Venus gradually shrink in

WEST

PISCES
CETUS
PERSEUS
Pleiades
12 Feb
TAURUS
Aldebaran
ERIDANUS
Zenith
Capella
AURIGA
Castor
GEMINI
Pollux
15 Feb
ORION
Bellatrix
Mintaka
Alnilam
Betelgeuse
Alnitak
Orion Nebula
Rigel
Saiph
LEPUS
Mirzam
CANIS MAJOR
Adhara
Sirius
Procyon
CANIS MINOR
THE MILKY WAY
PUPPIS
SOUTH
SE
URSA MAJOR
The Sickle
CANCER
Regulus
18 Feb
LEO
HYDRA
VIRGO
Saturn
Ecliptic
EAST

February's Object
Orion Nebula

Saturn

Moon

| MOON | | |
|---|---|---|
| Date | Time | Phase |
| 3 | 2.30 am | New Moon |
| 11 | 7.18 am | First Quarter |
| 18 | 8.36 am | Full Moon |
| 24 | 11.26 pm | Last Quarter |

11

◄ *Robin Scagell took this picture of Comet Hale-Bopp using a 35 mm camera with 135 mm telephoto lens mounted on a driven equatorial mount — there was no telescope involved. The exposure time was 5 minutes on ISO 1600 Ektachrome film on Good Friday, 29 March 1997, from a country location near Kingsbridge, Devon.*

size, while becoming more and more illuminated by the Sun.

**Mercury**, **Mars** and **Neptune** are all lost in the Sun's glare in February.

## MOON

On 6 and 7 February, the crescent Moon lies near Jupiter, low in the evening sky. The First Quarter Moon passes the Seven Sisters (Pleiades) star cluster on 11 February. On the night of 20/21 February, the Moon lies below Saturn, and on 21/22 February it passes Spica. It's near another bright star, Antares, just before dawn on 25 February, and you'll find the very thin crescent Moon next to Venus just before the Sun rises on 28 February.

## SPECIAL EVENTS

On **11 February**, the Moon lies just 1.5 degrees from the Pleiades star cluster, making a pretty grouping in the sky.

And on **14 February**, the Stardust space probe makes a flypast of Comet Tempel-1 (see this month's Topic).

## FEBRUARY'S OBJECT

Below Orion's Belt lies a small fuzzy patch. Through binoculars, or a small telescope, the patch looks like a small cloud in space. It *is* a cloud – but at 30 light years across, it's hardly petite. Only the distance of the **Orion Nebula** – 1300 light years – diminishes it. Yet it is the nearest region to Earth where heavyweight stars are being born: this 'star factory' contains at least 150 fledgling stars (protostars), which have condensed out of dark clouds of gas and dust.

The Orion Nebula, illuminated by the searing radiation from young stars, is a great sight through a telescope or binoculars – and even with the unaided eye from a dark location.

## FEBRUARY'S PICTURE

**Comet Hale-Bopp**, photographed on its spectacular appearance in spring 1997. The blue tail is caused by gas given off from the head, or nucleus, of the comet, while the yellowish tail is dust from the nucleus. A cousin to Tempel-1 – which the Stardust space probe will visit this month – this comet was one of the most sensational sky-sights in the past few years.

### ◉ *Viewing tip*

It may sound obvious, but if you want to stargaze at this most glorious time of year, dress up warmly! Lots of layers are better than a heavy coat, as they trap air next to your skin – and heavy-soled boots stop the frost creeping up your legs. It may sound anorakish, but a woolly hat really does stop one-third of your body's heat escaping through the top of your head. And, alas, no hipflask of whisky – alcohol constricts the veins, and makes you feel even colder.

## FEBRUARY'S TOPIC
### When Stardust meets Tempel-1...

Valentine's Day this year might be heavier on data, rather than on dates. On 14 February, the venerable Stardust space probe – which has been surveying the Solar System for over ten years – will get up close and personal to the comet Tempel-1. This icy piece of cosmic debris was the controversial victim of Deep Impact, a probe that explosively struck the comet with the intention of discovering its content and structure.

Stardust is no stranger to comets. In 2005, it visited the comet Wild 2, and collected dust samples which it returned to Earth. Now it will take images of the crater caused by Deep Impact and analyze the dust and gas that pour off this icy celestial wanderer, which orbits the Sun roughly every five years. The findings will prove to be interesting – for comets are the leftover building debris from the birth of our Solar System.

This month, the nights become shorter than the days as we hit the Vernal (Spring) Equinox – on 20 March, spring is 'official'. That's the date when the Sun climbs up over the Equator to shed its rays over the northern hemisphere. Because of the Earth's inclination of 23.5° to its orbital path around the Sun, the North Pole points away from our local star between September and March, causing the long nights of autumn and winter. Come the northern spring, Earth's axial tilt means that the Sun favours the north – and we can look forward to the long, warm days of summer.

Even better, the clocks 'spring forward' on 27 March, making daytime even longer.

### MARCH'S CONSTELLATION

**Canes Venatici** (the Hunting Dogs) has to be one of the most obscure constellations ever invented. It lies directly under the tail of the Great Bear (**Ursa Major**).

Brought into the cosmos by Johannes Hevelius, the great 17th-century Polish astronomer (and member of a brewing circle), the pair of faint stars making up the constellation represent Asterion and Chara, two dogs chasing the Great Bear around the pole. Asterion is more familiarly known today as **Cor Caroli** – Charles' Heart – named by Sir Charles Scarborough after the doomed king Charles I of England.

The constellation houses a gem, although you'll need a fairly mighty telescope to see it as more than just a fuzzy blur. It's the glorious Whirlpool Galaxy (**M51**) – a face-on spiral with a little companion hand-in-hand with it (see Picture). In 1845, Lord Rosse, of Birr Castle in Ireland, sketched the pair as he saw them through his telescope. The 'Leviathan of Parsonstown' – then the largest astronomical instrument in the world – boasted a 1.8-metre (72-inch) mirror and it was the first to reveal spiral structure in galaxies.

▼ *The sky at 10 pm in mid-March, with Moon positions at three-day intervals either side of Full Moon. The star positions are also correct for 11 pm at*

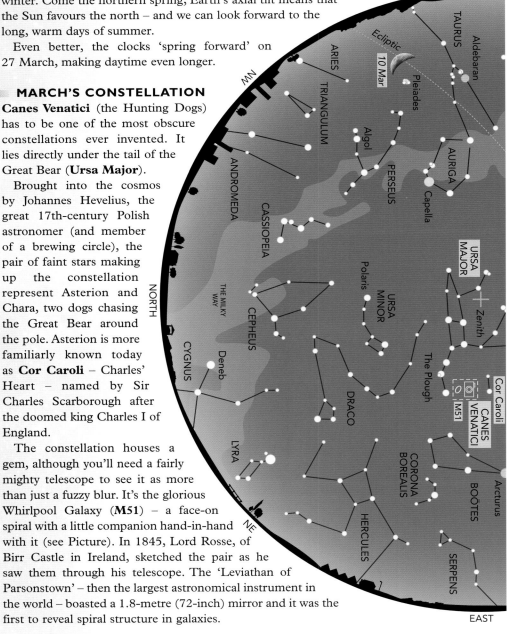

the beginning of March, and 10 pm at the end of the month (after BST begins). The planets move slightly relative to the stars during the month.

## PLANETS ON VIEW

It's our last chance this year to see great **Jupiter** in the evening sky, brilliant at magnitude −1.9 in the constellation Cetus (just outside the zodiacal constellation Pisces). At the beginning of March, Jupiter is setting around 8 pm, but by the end of the month it has totally sunk into the twilight glow.

During the second half of March, Jupiter is joined in the evening sky by tiny **Mercury**, putting on its best evening appearance of 2011 – it's at greatest eastern elongation on 23 March. You'll spot Mercury very low in the west about an hour and a half after sunset. When the innermost planet first hoves into sight, around 12 March, it shines at magnitude −1.1, but it fades rapidly to magnitude +1.7 by the end of the month. At first, you'll see Mercury to the lower right of Jupiter; the planets pass on 15 March (see Special Events), and then Mercury lies directly above Jupiter.

**Saturn** (magnitude +0.7) lies in Virgo. It rises at 8.45 pm at the beginning of March, and at 7.45 pm at the end of the month.

**Venus** rises in the south-east an hour or so before the Sun. At magnitude −3.9, the brilliant Morning Star is hard to miss, even though it's now down in the twilight glow and won't be visible in a dark sky again until November.

**Mars**, **Uranus** and **Neptune** are too close to the Sun to be seen this month.

## MOON

On the very first morning of the month, 1 March, the thin crescent Moon lies to

*Star chart labels:* WEST, Aldebaran, TAURUS, ERIDANUS, Rigel, ORION, Betelgeuse, LEPUS, 13 Mar, MS, Procyon, CANIS MINOR, THE MILKY WAY, CANIS MAJOR, AURIGA, GEMINI, Castor, Pollux, CANCER, PUPPIS, Zenith, URSA MAJOR, The Sickle, 16 Mar, Regulus, LEO, HYDRA, SOUTH, M51, CANES VENATICI, Cor Caroli, Denebola, Moon, 19 Mar, CORVUS, BOÖTES, Arcturus, Saturn, VIRGO, Spica, Ecliptic, SE, SERPENS, EAST

March's Object
The Moon

March's Picture
M51

Saturn

Moon

| MOON | | |
|---|---|---|
| **Date** | **Time** | **Phase** |
| 4 | 8.46 pm | New Moon |
| 12 | 11.45 pm | First Quarter |
| 19 | 6.10 pm | Full Moon |
| 26 | 12.07 pm | Last Quarter |

the left of Venus. The evening of 6 March sees the waxing crescent Moon to the right of Jupiter. On 10 March, the Moon lies near the Pleiades, and on 17 March it passes Regulus. You'll find the Moon below Saturn and to the right of Spica on 20 March. On the mornings of 24 and 25 March the Moon is near Antares. And on the very last morning of the month, 31 March, the crescent Moon is back with Venus, low in the dawn sky.

## SPECIAL EVENTS

On **15 March**, the Solar System's biggest world, Jupiter, lies next to the smallest planet, Mercury. Jupiter (to the left) appears about twice as bright as Mercury; in reality, it's almost 30 times wider, but it's currently over five times further away.

The Vernal (Spring) Equinox, on **20 March** at 11.21 pm, marks the beginning of spring, as the Sun moves up to shine over the northern hemisphere.

**27 March**, 1.00 am: British Summer Time starts – don't forget to put your clocks forward by an hour (the mnemonic is '*Spring* forward, *Fall* back').

◉ **Viewing tip**

This is the time of year to tie down your compass points – the directions of north, south, east and west as seen from your observing site. North is easy – just latch on to Polaris, the Pole Star. And at noon, the Sun is always in the south. But the useful extra in March is that we hit the Spring Equinox, when the Sun rises due east, and sets due west. So remember those positions relative to a tree or house around your horizon.

## MARCH'S OBJECT

The **Moon** is our nearest celestial companion, lying a mere 384,400 kilometres away. It took the Apollo astronauts only three days to reach it! And at 3476 kilometres across, it's so large when compared to Earth that – from space – the system would look like a double planet.

But the Moon couldn't be more different from our verdant Earth. Bereft of an atmosphere, it has been exposed to bombardment by meteorites and asteroids throughout its life. Even with the unaided eye, you can see the evidence. The 'face' of the 'Man in the Moon' consists of huge craters created by asteroid hits 3.8 billion years ago.

Through binoculars or a telescope, the surface of the Moon looks amazing – as if you're flying over it. But don't observe our satellite when it's Full: the light is flat and swamps its features. It's best to roam the Moon when it's a crescent and see the sideways-on shadows highlighting its dramatic relief.

## MARCH'S PICTURE

**M51**, the Whirlpool Galaxy, is one of the most beautiful sky-sights – but it's the result of a cosmic traffic accident. Hundreds of millions of years ago, the small companion galaxy (seen above) collided with its larger neighbour, leading to a burst of starbirth in the Whirlpool. As a result, its glorious spiral arms are cradling young stars.

## MARCH'S TOPIC
### Messenger to the gods

Look out for elusive Mercury this month. Rumour has it that the architect of our Solar System – Nicolaus Copernicus – never observed the tiny world because of mists rising from the nearby River Vistula in Poland.

The pioneering space probe Mariner 10 sent back only fleeting images as it swung past the diminutive, cratered planet 35 years ago. But on 18 March, all is to change, for that's when NASA's Messenger probe goes into orbit around Mercury.

Messenger (the convoluted acronym stands for ME-rcury S-urface S-pace EN-vironment GE-ochemistry and R-anging mission) celebrates the belief that, in mythology, fleet-footed Mercury was messenger to the gods. Messenger has already made three flybys of Mercury, to slow down the probe so that it can enter Mercury's orbit this month. By then, Messenger will have travelled almost 8 billion kilometres and made 15 circuits around the Sun.

Once in Mercury-orbit, Messenger's suite of instruments will scan the planet's surface and scrutinize its composition, offering a clue to the origins of this mysterious body – which may have been born further out from the Sun and later spiralled in. Messenger will also explore Mercury's internal workings – and it could confirm news of the latest discovery from Earth: that our innermost world has a core made of molten iron.

This enigmatic little planet will later be the target for the European probe BepiColombo, to be launched in 2013. BepiColombo comes in two parts: a Japanese spacecraft orbiting high above Mercury to probe its magnetism, and a European orbiter to examine its surface in extreme close-up.

◀ *Spiral galaxy M51 (the Whirlpool Galaxy) photographed by Eddie Guscott from Corringham, Essex, using a C9.25 Schmidt-Cassegrain telescope (235 mm aperture) on 25 March 2007. The total exposure time through separate colour filters was 3½ hours.*

The ancient constellations of **Leo** and **Virgo** dominate the springtime skies. Leo does indeed look like a recumbent lion, but it's hard to envisage Virgo as anything other than a vast 'Y' in the sky!

When you're looking at Virgo, spot the interloper. It's the planet Saturn, closest to the Earth this month. 'Close', however, is relative: the ringworld is over a billion kilometres distant.

*▼ The sky at 11 pm in mid-April, with Moon positions at three-day intervals either side of Full Moon. The star positions are also correct for midnight at the beginning of*

## APRIL'S CONSTELLATION

The Y-shaped constellation of **Virgo** is the second-largest in the sky. It takes a bit of imagination to see the group of stars as a virtuous maiden holding an ear of corn (the bright star **Spica**), but this very old constellation has associations with the times of harvest. In the early months of autumn, the Sun passes through the stars of Virgo, hence the connections with the gathering-in of fruit and wheat.

Spica is a hot, blue-white star over 13,000 times brighter than the Sun, boasting a temperature of 22,500°C. It has a stellar companion, which lies just 18 million kilometres away from Spica – closer than Mercury orbits the Sun. Both stars inflict a mighty gravitational toll on each other, raising huge tides – thus creating two distorted, egg-shaped stars. Spica is the celestial equivalent of a rugby ball.

The glory of Virgo is the 'bowl' of the Y-shape. Scan it with a small telescope, and, you'll find it packed with faint, fuzzy blobs. These are just a few of the 2000 galaxies – star-cities like the Milky Way – that make up the gigantic **Virgo Cluster** (see Picture).

## PLANETS ON VIEW

It's a pretty poor month for planet-lovers. Brilliant **Venus** (magnitude −3.8) is skulking in the dawn twilight: you may catch it just before sunrise low in the east.

*April, and 10 pm at the end of the month. The planets move slightly relative to the stars during the month.*

Otherwise, the only planet you'll see is **Saturn**. With the dark skies to itself, the ringworld is putting on its most magnificent display of the year, shining all night long at magnitude +0.6 in the constellation Virgo. On 3 April, Saturn is at opposition, closest to our planet – a 'mere' 1290 million kilometres away – and opposite the Sun as seen from Earth.

If you watch the planet carefully through a telescope from the beginning of April until the end of the month, you'll notice that the rings are significantly brighter around opposition. Saturn's gaudy appendages are made of icy particles that reflect light back towards the Sun (like motorway signs glaring in our car headlights), and this beam of reflected light is directed towards Earth when Saturn is opposite to the Sun in our skies.

**Mercury**, **Mars**, **Jupiter**, **Uranus** and **Neptune** are lost in the Sun's glare this month.

### MOON

On 7 April, the crescent Moon lies near the Pleiades, low in the north-west. The Moon passes below Regulus on the night of 13/14 April, Saturn on 16 April and Spica on 17 April. You'll spot the Moon near Antares on the morning of 21 April. The thin crescent Moon lies above Venus just before dawn on 30 April.

### SPECIAL EVENTS

**22/23 April**: It's the maximum of the **Lyrid** meteor shower, which – by perspective – appears to emanate from the constellation of Lyra. The

WEST

THE MILKY WAY

GEMINI

Procyon

CANIS MINOR

CANCER

12 Apr

Castor

Pollux

URSA MAJOR

Zenith

Regulus

LEO

Denebola

HYDRA

S

M84/M86

Virgo Cluster

15 Apr

CORVUS

CANES VENATICI

Arcturus

SOUTH

The Plough

CORONA BOREALIS

BOÖTES

SERPENS

VIRGO

Saturn

Ecliptic

Spica

18 Apr

LIBRA

HERCULES

OPHIUCHUS

SE

EAST

April's Picture
Virgo Cluster

Saturn

Moon

| MOON | | |
|------|------|-------|
| Date | Time | Phase |
| 3 | 3.32 pm | New Moon |
| 11 | 1.05 pm | First Quarter |
| 18 | 3.44 am | Full Moon |
| 25 | 3.47 am | Last Quarter |

shower consists of particles from Comet Thatcher. It will be best to look for Lyrids after 2 am, when the Moon has set.

*▲ This photograph of the Virgo Cluster was taken by Eddie Guscott using a 130 mm refractor from Corringham, Essex, with a total exposure time of 5 hours 10 minutes through separate colour filters.*

## APRIL'S OBJECT

The **Sun** is livening up – and in more ways than one. As spring progresses, our local star climbs higher in the sky, and we feel the warmth of its rays. Some 150 million kilometres away, the Sun is our local star – and our local nuclear reactor.

This giant ball of hydrogen gas is a vast hydrogen bomb. At its core, where temperatures reach 15.7 million degrees, the Sun fuses atoms of hydrogen into helium. Every second, it devours 4 million tonnes of itself, bathing the Solar System with light and warmth.

But the Sun is also a dangerous place. It's now emerging from a quiet period to become active again; a cycle that repeats roughly 11 years. The driver is the Sun's magnetic field, wound up by the spinning of our star's surface gases. The magnetic activity suppresses the Sun's circulation, leading to a rash of dark sunspots. Then the pent-up energy is released in a frenzy of activity, when our star hurls charged particles through the Solar System. These dangerous particles can kill satellites, and even disrupt power lines on Earth. And if we are ever to make the three-year human journey to Mars, we will have to take the Sun's unpredictable, malevolent weather into account.

## APRIL'S PICTURE

Markarian's Chain, a line of galaxies in the **Virgo Cluster**, with the galaxies **M86** (centre) and **M84** (right). The Virgo Cluster of galaxies, 50 million light years away, dominates our place in the Universe. These huge, impressive galaxies – around 2000 of them – are the centre of our own local supercluster of galaxies. This massive agglomeration controls its galactic neighbourhood for millions of light years.

## APRIL'S TOPIC
### Saturn

The slowly moving ringworld **Saturn** is currently skulking in the peripheries of the sprawling constellation **Virgo** (the Virgin). It's famed for its huge engirdling appendages: the rings would stretch nearly all the way from the Earth to the Moon.

And the rings are just the beginnings of Saturn's larger family. It has at least 60 moons, including Titan – where the international Cassini-Huygens mission has discovered lakes of liquid methane and ethane. And the latest news is that Cassini has imaged plumes of salty water spewing from Saturn's icy moon Enceladus.

Saturn itself is second only to Jupiter in size. But it's so low in density that were you to plop it in an ocean, it would float. Like Jupiter, Saturn has a ferocious spin rate – 10 hours and 32 minutes – and its winds roar at speeds of up to 1800 km/h.

Saturn's atmosphere is much blander than that of its larger cousin. But it's wracked with lightning-bolts 1000 times more powerful than those on Earth.

Look up towards the south and you'll spot a distinctly orange-coloured star that lords it over a huge area of sky devoid of other bright stars. This is **Arcturus**, the brightest star in the constellation of **Boötes** (the Herdsman), who shepherds the two bears through the heavens. A sure sign that summer is on the way!

▼ *The sky at 11 pm in mid-May, with Moon positions at three-day intervals either side of Full Moon. The star positions are also correct for midnight at the beginning of*

## MAY'S CONSTELLATION

**Boötes** (the Herdsman) is shaped rather like a kite. It was mentioned in Homer's Odyssey, and its name refers to the fact that Boötes seems to 'herd' the stars that lie in the northern part of the sky.

The name of the brightest star, **Arcturus**, means 'bear-driver'. It apparently 'drives' the Great Bear (**Ursa Major**) around the sky as the Earth rotates. Arcturus is the fourth brightest star in the whole sky, and it's the most brilliant star you can see on May evenings. A red giant star (see Topic) in its old age, Arcturus lies 37 light years from us, and shines 110 times more brilliantly than the Sun.

The star at the ten o'clock position from Arcturus is called **Izar**, whose name means 'the belt'. Through a good telescope, it appears as a gorgeous double star – one star is yellow and the other blue.

## PLANETS ON VIEW

The spring 2011 planetary drought continues into May. The noble exception is **Saturn**, still strutting its stuff in the constellation Virgo. Visible all night long in the south, the ringworld shines at magnitude +0.8, and is gradually moving towards Porrima, the star marking the centre of the Y-shaped constellation.

Telescope-users can now spot distant **Neptune** (magnitude +7.9) in Aquarius, rising in the south-east around 2.30 am.

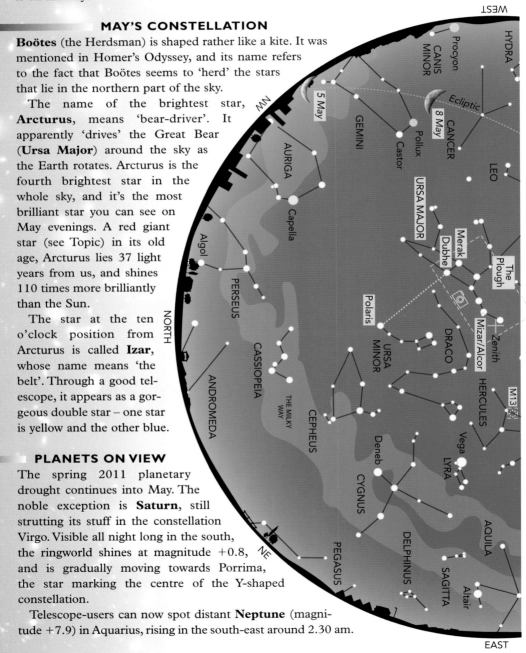

*May, and 10 pm at the end of the month. The planets move slightly relative to the stars during the month.*

**Venus** is skulking low on the south-eastern horizon an hour before sunrise, but even at a brilliant magnitude −3.8 you'll need to know exactly where to look to catch it in the dawn twilight.

It will be equally difficult to spot **Jupiter**, when it begins to rise from the sunrise glow in the last few days of May. Making its debut an hour and a half before the Sun, the giant planet shines at magnitude −2.0 in Pisces, lying to the right of Venus.

**Mercury** (at western elongation on 7 May), **Mars** and **Uranus** are too close to the Sun to be seen this month.

## MOON

The Moon lies near Regulus on 11 May. On 13 May, it passes below Saturn, and on 14 May the Moon is near Spica. On 17 and 18 May, the star keeping the Moon company low in the south is Antares. The crescent Moon lies immediately above Jupiter just before dawn on 29 May, and next to Venus on the morning of 31 May.

## SPECIAL EVENTS

The maximum of the Eta Aquarid meteor shower falls on **4/5 May**, when tiny pieces of Halley's Comet burn up in Earth's atmosphere. Because the Moon is well out of the way, 2011 is a good year for observing these shooting stars.

## MAY'S OBJECT

At the darkest part of a May night, you may spot a faint fuzzy patch in **Hercules**, up high in the

WEST

CANCER
Regulus
The Sickle
HYDRA
MS
11 May
URSA MAJOR
LEO
CORVUS
The Plough
CANES VENATICI
Saturn
14 May
Mizar/Alcor
Zenith
BOÖTES
Izar
Arcturus
VIRGO
Spica
CENTAURUS
SOUTH
HYDRA
M13
CORONA BOREALIS
SERPENS
Ecliptic
LIBRA
HERCULES
OPHIUCHUS
17 May
AQUILA
THE MILKY WAY
SCORPIUS
Antares
SE
Altair
SERPENS

EAST

May's Object M13
May's Picture The Plough

Saturn
Moon

| MOON | | |
| --- | --- | --- |
| Date | Time | Phase |
| 3 | 7.51 am | New Moon |
| 10 | 9.33 pm | First Quarter |
| 17 | 12.09 pm | Full Moon |
| 24 | 7.52 pm | Last Quarter |

south. Through binoculars, it appears as a gently glowing ball of light. With a telescope, you can glimpse its true nature: a cluster of almost a million stars, swarming together in space.

This wonderful object is known as **M13**, because it was the 13th entry in the catalogue of fuzzy objects recorded by the 18th-century French astronomer Charles Messier. We now classify M13 as a 'globular cluster'. These great round balls of stars are among the oldest objects in our Milky Way Galaxy, dating back to its birth some 13 billion years ago.

In 1974, radio astronomers sent a message towards M13, hoping to inform the inhabitants of any planet there of our existence. There's only one problem: M13 lies so far away that we wouldn't receive a reply until AD 52,200!

## MAY'S PICTURE

**The Plough** is our best-loved constellation – always visible, always circling the Pole Star. Children call it 'the Saucepan' – to Americans it's 'the Big Dipper'. And earlier generations dubbed it 'Charles' Wain'. Officially, it's part of **Ursa Major** (the Great Bear). Look out for the double star, **Mizar** and **Alcor**, in the bend of the bear's tail (see June's Object).

### ⊙ *Viewing tip*

When you first go out to observe, you may be disappointed at how few stars you can see in the sky. But wait for around 20 minutes, and you'll be amazed at how your night vision improves. One reason for this 'dark adaption' is that the pupil of your eye gets larger to make the best of the darkness. More importantly, in dark conditions the retina of your eye builds up much bigger reserves of rhodopsin, the chemical that responds to light.

You can use the two 'end' stars of the Plough (**Merak** and **Dubhe**) to locate **Polaris**. Draw a line between these two 'pointers', and extend it to hit the Pole Star (see chart on page 22).

---

**MAY'S TOPIC**
**Red giants**

**Arcturus**, the fourth-brightest star in the sky (magnitude −0.04) always gladdens our hearts as the harbinger of summer's arrival. But, alas, it is a star on the way out. Its orange colour indicates that it's a red giant: a star near the end of its life.

Arcturus is about 30 times wider than the Sun – even though it comes in at the same weight – because it has swollen up in its old age. This is a fate that not only befalls humans, it also happens to stars (although the causes are rather different!). Stars generate energy by nuclear fusion: they 'burn' hydrogen into the next-up element, helium, in their hot cores.

But there's only a finite supply of hydrogen in a star's core. When it runs out – after around 10 billion years – the core, made of helium, collapses to a smaller size and gets even hotter. The star is now like an onion, with distinct layers. In the centre, the compressed helium switches on its own reactions. And there's a layer around the core, where hydrogen is still turning to helium. These reactions create more heat, causing the outer layers of the star to balloon in size and cool down – hence the baleful red or orange colour of the star's surface.

Eventually Arcturus, like all red giants, will lose the grip on its atmosphere and jettison it into space, as a glowing planetary nebula (see June's Topic). All that's left will be the dying core: a steadily cooling object, about the size of the Earth, called a white dwarf. This fate awaits our Sun – but not for another 7 billion years.

◀ *The Plough, photographed on Ektachrome 1600 film by Robin Scagell. He used a 1-minute exposure through a 58 mm lens with a diffusion filter in front which expanded the larger star images, bringing out their colour.*

This month, our local star reaches its highest position over the northern hemisphere, when we get the longest days and shortest nights. The Summer Solstice this year takes place on 21 June, and the height of summer will no doubt be celebrated at festivals around the northern hemisphere on this day – notably at Stonehenge, in Wiltshire. This seasonal ritual traces its roots back through millennia, and has led to the construction of massive stone monuments aligned on the rising Sun at midsummer. Our ancestors clearly had formidable astronomical knowledge.

### JUNE'S CONSTELLATION

**Lyra** is one of the most perfect little constellations in the sky. Shaped like a Greek lyre, it's dominated by brilliant white **Vega**, the fifth-brightest star in the sky. Just 25 light years away – a near-neighbour in the Cosmos – Vega is surrounded by a disc of dust that has probably given birth to baby planets.

Next to Vega is **epsilon Lyrae**, a quadruple star known as the 'double-double'. Keen-sighted people can separate the pair, but you'll need a small telescope to find that each star is itself double.

The gem of Lyra lies between the two end stars of the constellation, **beta** and **gamma Lyrae**. This one needs a serious telescope, as it's nearly 9th magnitude. The **Ring Nebula** is a cosmic smoke-ring: the end of the life for a star like the Sun. We explore these beautiful, but grim, cosmic corpses on page 29 (see Topic).

### PLANETS ON VIEW

**Saturn** lords it over the evening sky, at magnitude +0.9 in Virgo. All month long, the ringed planet lies very near Porrima, the star at the centre of the constellation's

▼ *The sky at 11 pm in mid-June, with Moon positions at three-day intervals either side of Full Moon. The star positions are also correct for midnight at the beginning of*

WEST

Ecliptic

6 June

Regulus

The Sickle

CANCER

LEO

Pollux

NW

Castor

GEMINI

URSA MAJOR

CANES VENATICI

Dubhe

The Plough

Alkaid

AURIGA

Mizar/ Alcor

HERCULES

Zenith

Capella

URSA MINOR

DRACO

M92

NORTH

Polaris

Vega
epsilon LYRA

beta
gamma

CASSIOPEIA

CEPHEUS

PERSEUS

THE MILKY WAY

Deneb

CYGNUS

Algol

Andromeda

NE

Square of Pegasus

PEGASUS

DELPHINUS

EAST

*June, and 10 pm at the end of the month. The planets move slightly relative to the stars during the month.*

Y-shape. Soon after Saturn sets in the west around 2 am, a brighter challenger rises in the east: **Jupiter** (magnitude −2.0), blazing among the faint stars of Pisces and Aries.

The two more distant giant planets are also to be found in June's night sky. **Neptune** (magnitude +7.9) rises about 0.30 am: this telescopic world is inhabiting Aquarius. At magnitude +5.9, **Uranus** is technically visible to the naked eye – but certainly not in June's bright summer nights! Uranus lies in Pisces and rises about 1.30 am.

**Venus** is still horizon-hugging in the dawn twilight, a lone light in the brightening sky, at magnitude −3.8. And, in the last week of June, **Mars** emerges at long last from the glare of the Sun's light. You'll find the Red Planet in Taurus, rising in the north-east just before 3 am – although at only magnitude +1.3 it's not yet making much of a statement.

**Mercury** is the only planet too close to the Sun to be seen in June.

### MOON

On 7 June, the waxing Moon lies near Regulus, while 10 June sees the Moon passing below Saturn. On 11 June, the Moon is near Spica. The almost Full Moon lies right above Antares on 14 June. In the early hours of 26 June, the crescent Moon is next to Jupiter. Just before dawn on 28 and 29 June, the narrow crescent is near Mars (the Pleiades are just above, but will be difficult to spot in the twilight).

WEST

LEO
9 June
Saturn
VIRGO
CORVUS
Spica
MS
HYDRA
URSA MAJOR
CANES VENATICI
BOÖTES
Arcturus
CORONA BOREALIS
SERPENS
LIBRA
12 June
SCORPIUS
SOUTH
Alkaid
The Plough
DRACO
Zenith
M92
HERCULES
OPHIUCHUS
Ecliptic
Vega
epsilon
beta
LYRA
gamma
Ring Nebula
SAGITTA
SERPENS
SAGITTARIUS
15 June
CYGNUS
Altair
AQUILA
THE MILKY WAY
PEGASUS
DELPHINUS
AQUARIUS
CAPRICORNUS
SE

EAST

June's Objects
Mizar and Alcor

June's Picture
M92

Saturn

Moon

| MOON | | |
|------|------|-------|
| Date | Time | Phase |
| 1 | 10.02 pm | New Moon |
| 9 | 3.11 am | First Quarter |
| 15 | 9.13 pm | Full Moon |
| 23 | 11.48 pm | Last Quarter |

▲ *Globular cluster M92 in Hercules, photographed by Eddie Guscott using a 130 mm refracting telescope from Corringham, Essex, on 28 April 2006. The total CCD exposure time through separate red, green and blue colour filters was 2 hours 20 minutes.*

## SPECIAL EVENTS

There's a partial eclipse of the Sun on **1 June**, but you'll need to be somewhere around the Arctic Ocean to see anything of it.

**21 June**, 6.16 pm: Summer Solstice. The Sun reaches its most northerly point in the sky, so 21 June is Midsummer's Day, with the longest period of daylight. Correspondingly, we have the shortest nights.

We're due for an eclipse of the Moon on **15 June**, total as seen from the UK – but unfortunately not in a dark sky. The Moon is totally eclipsed when it rises in the south-east at 9.20 pm, but, with the bright dusk sky, you won't see it at all. The Moon starts to move out of the Earth's shadow at 10.00 pm, and returns to Full Moon glory by 11.00 pm.

## JUNE'S OBJECT

Home in on the 'kink' in the tail of **Ursa Major** (the Great Bear), and you'll spot the most famous pair of stars in the sky – **Mizar** (magnitude +2.4) and **Alcor** (magnitude +4.0). Generations of astronomers have referred to them as 'the horse and rider', and students have been raised on the fact that the pair make up a classic double star system, orbiting in each other's embrace. But *are* Mizar and Alcor an item? It seems not. Although they both lie about 80 light years away, they are separated by 3 light years – nearly the distance from the Sun to our closest star, Proxima Centauri. Undoubtedly, Mizar is a complex star system, having a companion visible through a telescope which is itself double; in total, there are four stars involved. But it appears that Alcor is an innocent bystander. Although it shares its path through space with Mizar, the two are just members of most of the stars that make up the 'stellar association' of Ursa Major. Unlike most constellations, the stars of the Great Bear are genuinely linked by birth (with the exceptions of **Dubhe** and **Alkaid**, at opposite ends of the central '**Plough**'). So let's hear 'independence for Alcor'!

## JUNE'S PICTURE

**M92** is a globular cluster of some 330,000 stars located at the top of the constellation of **Hercules**. It is overshadowed by its brighter neighbour M13 (see May's Object), but it is nevertheless a lovely cluster. In crystal-clear skies, M92 is just visible to the unaided eye. It was discovered in 1777 by Johann Bode. Lying 26,000 light years away, M92 is one of an estimated 158 globular clusters – all made of ancient stars – that live in the outer 'halo' of our Galaxy.

## JUNE'S TOPIC
### Planetary nebulae

William Herschel – who discovered the planet Uranus – first named these fuzzy objects 'planetary nebulae', because, to him, they looked like the planet that he had found. Now we know that they are the end-point for the majority of stars.

When a star like the Sun runs out of its nuclear fuel at the end of its life, its core – in a desperate attempt to keep the star alive – contracts, heating up its outer layers. The star becomes unstable and puffs off its atmosphere into space in the shape of a ring.

The ring disperses in a few thousand years. It leaves the derelict core inside to leak away its energy – ending up as a cold, lonely black dwarf.

The most famous planetary nebula in the sky is the **Ring Nebula** in **Lyra** – a classic cosmic smoke-ring.

High summer is here, and with it comes the brilliant trio of the **Summer Triangle** – the stars **Vega**, **Deneb** and **Altair**. Each is the brightest star in its own constellation: Vega in **Lyra**, Deneb in **Cygnus**, and Altair in **Aquila**. And this is the time to catch the far-southern constellations of **Sagittarius** and **Scorpius** – embedded in the glorious heart of the Milky Way.

▼ *The sky at 11 pm in mid-July, with Moon positions at three-day intervals either side of Full Moon. The star positions are also correct for midnight at the beginning of*

## JULY'S CONSTELLATION

Low down in the south, you'll find a constellation that's shaped rather like a teapot – **Sagittarius**. The handle lies to the left and the spout to the right!

To the ancient Greeks, the star-pattern of Sagittarius represented an archer, with the torso of a man and the body of a horse. The 'handle' of the teapot represents his upper body, the curve of three stars to the right are his bent bow, while the end of the spout is the point of the arrow, aimed at **Scorpius**, the fearsome celestial scorpion.

Sagittarius is rich with nebulae and star clusters. If you have a clear night (and preferably from a southern latitude), sweep Sagittarius with binoculars for some fantastic sights. Above the spout lies the wonderful **Lagoon Nebula** – visible to the naked eye on clear nights. This is a region where stars are being born. Between the teapot and the neighbouring constellation **Aquila**, you'll find a bright patch of stars in the Milky Way (catalogued as **M24**). Raise your binoculars higher to spot another star-forming region, the **Omega Nebula**.

Finally, on a very dark night you may spot a fuzzy patch, above and to the left of the teapot's lid. This is the globular cluster **M22**, a swarm of almost a million stars that lies 10,000 light years away.

WEST

NW

The Sickle

LEO

VIRGO

BOÖTES

CANES VENATICI

The Plough

HERCULES

URSA MAJOR

URSA MINOR

DRACO

Zenith

CYGNUS

AURIGA

NORTH

Polaris

Deneb

Capella

CASSIOPEIA

CEPHEUS

THE MILKY WAY

North America Nebula

PERSEUS

Algol

PEGASUS

Square of Pegasus

TRIANGULUM

ANDROMEDA

NE

PISCES

EAST

*July, and 10 pm at the end of the month. The planets move slightly relative to the stars during the month.*

## PLANETS ON VIEW

The planetary scene is fairly humming again, after the doldrums of the past few months. During the first week of July, you may just catch **Mercury** (magnitude −0.1) very low in the north-west around 10.30 pm; it reaches greatest elongation on 20 July, past the time of best visibility.

During the evening, **Saturn** is the major planet on view. Shining at magnitude +1.0 in Virgo, close to the star Porrima, it's now setting around midnight.

**Neptune** (magnitude +7.8) lies in Aquarius and rises about 10.30 pm. It's followed by slightly brighter **Uranus**, just on naked-eye visibility at magnitude +5.8, rising at around 11.30 pm in Pisces.

If you wait up until 1 am, you can't miss glorious **Jupiter** rising in the east in the neighbouring constellation of Aries. The giant planet is the brightest object in July's night sky (after the Moon), at magnitude −2.2.

**Mars** rises just after 2 am, and you may catch it low in the north-east before the sky brightens. The Red Planet lies in Taurus, and shines at magnitude +1.4.

Rising just an hour before the Sun, at around 4 am, **Venus** (magnitude −3.8) is very difficult to spot in the dawn twilight.

## MOON

On 3 July, the thin crescent Moon lies to the left of Mercury – in the twilight sky, the view is best with binoculars. On 7 July, the Moon is below Saturn, and on 8 July

WEST

6 July

Saturn

VIRGO

Spica

9 July

LIBRA

Arcturus

BOÖTES

CORONA BOREALIS

SERPENS

SCORPIUS

12 July

Antares

DRACO

Zenith

OPHIUCHUS

SERPENS

M24

Lagoon Nebula

Vega

LYRA

HERCULES

SAGITTA

Omega Nebula

M22

SOUTH

Deneb

CYGNUS

SUMMER TRIANGLE

THE MILKY WAY

SAGITTARIUS

North America Nebula

AQUILA

Altair

15 July

PEGASUS

DELPHINUS

CAPRICORNUS

Neptune

PISCES

18 July

AQUARIUS

Ecliptic

SE

EAST

| | July's Object Summer Triangle | Saturn |
| | | Neptune |
| | July's Picture North America Nebula | Moon |

| MOON | | |
|---|---|---|
| **Date** | **Time** | **Phase** |
| 1 | 9.54 am | New Moon |
| 8 | 7.29 am | First Quarter |
| 15 | 7.39 am | Full Moon |
| 23 | 6.02 am | Last Quarter |
| 30 | 7.40 pm | New Moon |

the First Quarter Moon passes Spica. The Moon is near Antares on 11 and 12 July. In the morning of 24 July, the Moon is immediately above Jupiter. The crescent Moon lies near Mars on the mornings of 27 and 28 July.

### SPECIAL EVENTS

There's a tiny partial eclipse of the Sun on **1 July**, but you need to be near Antarctica to see it at all!

On **4 July**, the Earth is at aphelion, its furthest point from the Sun.

### JULY'S OBJECT

The **Summer Triangle** is very much part of this season's skies (and it hangs around for most of the autumn, too!). It's made up of Vega, Deneb and Altair – the brightest stars in the constellations of Lyra, Cygnus and Aquila, respectively. The trio of stars make a striking pattern almost overhead on July nights.

The stars may seem to be almost the same brightness, but they're very different beasts. **Altair** – its name means 'flying eagle' – is one of the Sun's nearest neighbours, at a distance of nearly 17 light years. It's about ten times brighter than the Sun and spins at a breakneck rate of once every 6.5 hours – as compared to around 30 days for our local star.

**Vega**, just over 25 light years away, is a brilliant white star nearly twice as hot as the Sun. In 1850, it was the first star to be photographed. Now, more sensitive instruments have revealed that Vega is surrounded by a dusty disc, which may be a planetary system in the process of formation.

While **Deneb** – meaning 'tail' (of the swan) – may appear to be the faintest of the trio, the reality is different. It lies a staggering 3200 light years away (a newly-measured distance from the Hipparcos satellite). To appear so bright in our skies, it must be truly luminous. We now know that Deneb is over 200,000 times brighter than our Sun – one of the most brilliant stars known.

### JULY'S PICTURE

The aptly-named **North America Nebula**, with its companion, the Pelican Nebula, lies next to brilliant Deneb in Cygnus. They are actually part of a single enormous cloud of gas and dust, poised to create generations of new stars. The gap between them is caused by intervening dark interstellar dust. The nebula glows red, the result of heating from a nearby star. Researchers suspect that it could well be Deneb. If this is the case, the nebulae are about 1800 light years away – and the North America Nebula measures a staggering 100 light years across.

▶ *Philip Perkins photographed the North America Nebula from Wiltshire through a 400 mm telephoto lens mounted on top of a driven telescope. He combined four separate 40-minute exposures on Ektapress film.*

◉ **Viewing tip**

This is the month when you really need a good, unobstructed view to the southern horizon to make out the summer constellations of Scorpius and Sagittarius. They never rise high in temperate latitudes, so make the best of a southerly view – especially over the sea – if you're away on holiday. A good southern horizon is also best for views of the planets, because they rise highest when they're in the south.

### JULY'S TOPIC
### DAWN at Vesta

This may seem like *déjà vu*: yes, we did feature the DAWN mission to the asteroids in *Stargazing 2006*. But the mission was postponed, cancelled, and then reinstated. This month, however, the daring NASA mission will reach its first target, the brightest asteroid, Vesta; the second is Ceres, the biggest asteroid (930 kilometres across). It will orbit each asteroid for a year or more, to check them out at close quarters. The mission's aim is to investigate the formation and evolution of our Solar System. Asteroids and comets are the building-blocks of planets, and give us clues to our origins – perhaps even the origin of life. The two asteroids couldn't be more different, which is why NASA has chosen them as targets. Ceres evolved with water present – there may even be frost or water vapour on its surface today. Vesta, on the other hand, originated in hot and violent circumstances. By studying the two asteroids, DAWN will be looking back to the earliest days of our Solar System.

Well, it should have been the Glorious Twelfth for astronomers this month: 12/13 August is the maximum of the **Perseid** meteor shower. But this year it's drowned out by moonlight. However – never fret! You can use the warm nights to take in a fine display of summer stars, and – this year – a great gathering of planets in the west.

▼ *The sky at 11 pm in mid-August, with Moon positions at three-day intervals either side of Full Moon. The star positions are also correct for midnight*

### AUGUST'S CONSTELLATION

The cosmic dragon writhes between the two bears in the northern sky. **Draco** is probably associated with Hercules' 12 labours, because its head rests on the (upside-down) superhero's feet. In this case, Hercules had to get past a crowd of nymphs and slay a 100-headed dragon (called Ladon) before completing his task – which, in this case, was stealing the immortal golden apples from the gardens of the Hesperides.

Confusingly, the brightest star in Draco is gamma Draconis – which ought to be third in the pecking order. Also known as **Eltanin**, this orange star shines at magnitude +2.2 and lies 148 light years away. But all this is to change: in 1.5 million years, it will swing past the Earth at a distance of 28 light years, outshining even Sirius.

Alpha Draconis (also known as **Thuban**), which by rights should be the brightest in the constellation, stumbles in at a mere magnitude +3.7. Thuban lies just below Ursa Minor, in the tail of the dragon, 300 light years away.

But what Thuban lacks in brightness, it makes up for in fame. Thuban was our Pole Star in the years around 2800 BC. It actually lay closer to the celestial pole than Polaris does now – just 2.5 arcminutes, as opposed to 42 for Polaris.

The swinging of Earth's axis – like the toppling of a spinning top – takes place over a period of 26,000 years. 'Precession'

WEST

CANES VENATICI

Arcturus

BOÖTES

CORONA BOREALIS

NW

The Plough

HERCULES

URSA MAJOR

Thuban

DRACO

Eltanin

URSA MINOR

Zenith

Polaris

CYGNUS

Deneb

NORTH

CASSIOPEIA

CEPHEUS

PEGASUS

Capella

Radiant of Perseids

THE MILKY WAY

AURIGA

PERSEUS

ANDROMEDA

TRIANGULUM

Algol

ARIES

19 Aug

NE

Pleiades

Jupiter

Ecliptic

CETUS

PISCES

EAST

*at the beginning of August, and 10 pm at the end of the month. The planets move slightly relative to the stars during the month.*

means that the Earth's north pole points to a number of stars over the millennia, which we spin 'underneath' – so they appear stationary in the sky. Look forward to AD 14,000, when brilliant **Vega** will take over the pole!

## PLANETS ON VIEW

**Saturn** (magnitude +1.1) has been in the evening sky for so long it seems like a permanent feature, but by the end of August it has sunk into the twilight glow. At the beginning of the month, it's setting at 11 pm, but by month's end it has gone by 9 pm. Take this last chance to view the ringed planet, adorning the arms of Virgo.

Its more remote sibling, **Neptune** (magnitude +7.8), is at opposition on 22 August – when the most distant planet is a 'mere' 4350 million kilometres away. It's visible all night long (in a telescope) in Aquarius. A moderate telescope reveals its biggest moon, Triton.

**Uranus**, at magnitude +5.7, lies in Pisces and rises around 9.30 pm.

Giant planet **Jupiter** is rising about 10.45 pm, in Aries. It's gradually brightening as the Earth moves closer, and ends the month at magnitude −2.5.

**Mars** is considerably dimmer, at magnitude +1.4. The Red Planet rises around 1.45 am, and moves from Taurus to Gemini during August.

During the last few days of the month, you may catch **Mercury** very low in the east before sunrise.

WEST

LIBRA
SERPENS
CORONA BOREALIS
SCORPIUS
7 Aug
SW
OPHIUCHUS
HERCULES
DRACO
Eltanin
Vega
LYRA
SAGITTA
SERPENS
THE MILKY WAY
SAGITTARIUS
10 Aug
SOUTH
Zenith
Deneb
CYGNUS
Altair
AQUILA
DELPHINUS
CAPRICORNUS
ANDROMEDA
PEGASUS
13 Aug
Neptune
PISCIS AUSTRINUS
Square of Pegasus
16 Aug
Uranus
AQUARIUS
PISCES
Ecliptic
CETUS
SE

EAST

| | | |
|---|---|---|
| ● | | Jupiter |
| ● | | Uranus |
| ● | | Neptune |
| ● | | Moon |

□ August's Object Neptune

⬦ Radiant of Perseids

| **MOON** | | |
|---|---|---|
| **Date** | **Time** | **Phase** |
| 6 | 12.08 pm | First Quarter |
| 13 | 7.57 pm | Full Moon |
| 21 | 10.55 pm | Last Quarter |
| 29 | 4.04 am | New Moon |

Venus is the Sun's glare in August.

## MOON

The crescent Moon passes Saturn on 3 August, and Spica on 4 August. Antares is the star near the Moon on 7 and 8 August. On 19 and 20 August, you'll find the waning Moon near Jupiter. The Moon passes below the Pleiades on 21 August. In the mornings of 25 and 26 August, the crescent Moon is near Mars. The thin crescent lies to the upper right of Mercury just before dawn on 27 August.

## SPECIAL EVENTS

The maximum of the annual **Perseid** meteor shower falls on **12/13 August**, but this is a very poor year for observing them as brilliant moonlight will drown out all but the brightest meteors.

## AUGUST'S OBJECT

With Pluto having been demoted to the status of being a mere 'ice dwarf', **Neptune** is officially the most remote planet in our Solar System. It lies about 4500 million kilometres away from

◉ *Viewing tip*

We know it's not a good year – because of the bright moonlight – but there's no excuse for not having a Perseids party! Despite the Moon, you'll still see the brightest meteors. The ideal viewing equipment is your unaided eye, plus a sleeping bag and a lounger on the lawn.

the Sun – 30 times the Earth's distance – in the twilight zone of our family of worlds. The gas giant takes nearly 165 years to circle the Sun. It has just completed one 'Neptune year' since its discovery in 1846.

This month, Neptune is just visible through a small telescope low in Aquarius and at its closest this year on 22 August. But you need a space probe to get up close and personal to the planet. In 1989, Voyager 2 managed this. It discovered a turquoise world 17 times more massive than Earth, cloaked in clouds of methane and ammonia.

Neptune has a family of 13 moons – one of which, Triton, boasts erupting ice volcanoes. And, like the other outer worlds, it's encircled by rings of debris – although, in Neptune's case, they're very faint.

For a planet so far from the Sun, Neptune is amazingly frisky. Its core blazes at 7000°C – hotter than the surface of the Sun. This internal heat drives dramatic storms, and winds of 2000 km/h – the fastest in the Solar System.

## AUGUST'S PICTURE

Early August is usually a great time to see shooting stars. The **Perseids** – debris from Comet Swift-Tuttle – stream into the atmosphere and burn up at the rate of roughly one a minute. This year, bright moonlight will swamp the cosmic fireworks display, but we won't be able to overlook a meteor as bright as this one!

## AUGUST'S TOPIC
### Juno and NuSTAR missions

This month, two major launches are taking place to monitor very different environments in the Universe. On 5 August, NASA's Juno probe blasts off from Cape Canaveral in Florida. This solar-powered craft is bound for Jupiter, the biggest world in our Solar System. It will orbit the giant planet's poles 33 times, to investigate the gas-world's atmosphere, structure and awesome magnetic field.

Just ten days later – on 15 August – NASA will launch NuSTAR, a ground-breaking mission to search for the most extreme results of violence in the Universe. It will sniff out black holes, map the gruesome results of supernova explosions, and study the most devastating effects of exploding galaxies. Watch this space – from behind the sofa!

The month's wet weather is most likely with us again – and we have the star-patterns to match. **Aquarius** (the Water Carrier) is part of a group of aqueous star-patterns that include **Cetus** (the Sea Monster), **Capricornus** (the Sea Goat), **Pisces** (the Fishes), **Piscis Austrinus** (the Southern Fish) and **Delphinus** (the Dolphin). There's speculation that the ancient Babylonians associated this region with water because the Sun passed through this zone of the heavens during their rainy season, from February to March.

### SEPTEMBER'S CONSTELLATION

**Cetus** – the sky's pet sea monster – straggles below the barren square of **Pegasus**. Like its fellow constellation, it has very few stars of note – bar one. **Mira** ('The Wonderful') was discovered in 1596 by the astronomer David Fabricius.

Over an 11-month period, it varies in brightness alarmingly. Normally, it changes between magnitude +3 and magnitude +10, but in 1779 William Herschel observed it as being as bright as Arcturus, the fourth brightest star in the sky.

Mira is a distended red giant, unable to control its girth. At its faintest, it is only about as bright as our Sun, but it can swell to become 1500 times brighter. This 'star out of hell' is 700 times bigger than our local star, and would engulf all the planets as far out as Jupiter if it were to be placed in our Solar System. Its fate will be to puff off its unstable atmosphere, and turn into a planetary nebula (see June's Topic).

Mira should reach maximum in the last week of September – but bear in mind that variable stars are as predictable as cats!

### PLANETS ON VIEW

**Jupiter** is now rising in the east, in Aries, just as the sky grows

▼ The sky at 11 pm in mid-September, with Moon positions at three-day intervals either side of Full Moon. The star positions are also correct for midnight at *the beginning of September, and 10 pm at the end of the month. The planets move slightly relative to the stars during the month.*

dark, around 8.45 pm. At magnitude −2.6, the brilliant planet dominates the view all night long. Use binoculars or a small telescope to track the ever-changing pattern of its four brightest moons.

At magnitude +7.8, you'll certainly need optical aid to view **Neptune**. The most distant planet lies in the constellation Aquarius and sets at about 4.30 am.

Its slightly brighter twin, **Uranus** (magnitude +5.7), is at opposition on 25 September and is above the horizon all night. Technically visible to the naked eye – under perfectly dark and clear skies – it's more easily found in binoculars or a small telescope.

**Mars** rises about 1.20 am, at magnitude +1.3. During September, Mars moves from Gemini to Cancer, and at the end of the month it approaches the Praesepe star cluster.

In the dawn skies, you may catch elusive **Mercury** during the first half of September, very low in the east around 5 am. The tiny planet is at greatest western elongation on 3 September, and it brightens from magnitude +0.3 to −1.1 during the first two weeks of the month. On the morning of 9 September, Mercury passes close to Regulus.

**Venus** and **Saturn** lie too close to the Sun to be seen this month.

## MOON

On 4 September, the First Quarter Moon lies above Antares. The Moon is near Jupiter on 16 September. The morning of 23 September sees the waning crescent Moon next to Mars;

WEST

SERPENS
OPHIUCHUS
HERCULES
SERPENS
Vega
LYRA
CYGNUS
Deneb
Zenith
CEPHEUS
ANDROMEDA
TRIANGULUM
ARIES
PISCES
TAURUS
Jupiter
15 Sept
Mira
CETUS
ERIDANUS
EAST

Veil Nebula
SAGITTA
Altair
DELPHINUS
AQUILA
THE MILKY WAY
SAGITTARIUS
6 Sept
9 Sept
Neptune
PEGASUS
Square of Pegasus
12 Sept
Uranus
Ecliptic
AQUARIUS
CAPRICORNUS
PISCIS AUSTRINUS
GRUS
Fomalhaut
SOUTH
SE

| | Jupiter |
| | Uranus |
| | Neptune |
| | Moon |

September's Object
Uranus

September's Picture
Veil Nebula

| **MOON** | | |
|---|---|---|
| Date | Time | Phase |
| 4 | 6.39 pm | First Quarter |
| 12 | 10.26 am | Full Moon |
| 20 | 2.39 pm | Last Quarter |
| 27 | 12.09 pm | New Moon |

on the morning of 25 September, it's just below Regulus.

## SPECIAL EVENTS

On **8 September**, the GRAIL spacecraft heads off from Cape Canaveral towards the Moon. The Gravity Recovery and Interior Laboratory mission will investigate our satellite's structure from crust to core, and probe the evolution of our Moon.

It's the Autumn Equinox at 10.04 am on **23 September**. The Sun is over the Equator as it heads southwards in the sky, and day and night are equal.

## SEPTEMBER'S OBJECT

If you're very sharp-sighted and have extremely dark skies, you stand a chance of spotting **Uranus** – the most distant planet visible to the unaided eye. At magnitude +5.7 in Pisces, it's

▼ *The Veil Nebula in Cygnus, photographed through Peter Shah's 200 mm Newtonian reflector. He gave a total of 50 minutes' exposure time through red, green and blue filters.*

### ⊚ *Viewing tip*

It's best to view your favourite objects when they're well clear of the horizon. When you look low down, you're seeing through a large thickness of the atmosphere – which is always shifting and turbulent. It's like trying to observe the outside world from the bottom of a swimming pool! This turbulence makes the stars appear to twinkle. Low-down planets also twinkle – although to a lesser extent because they subtend tiny discs, and aren't so affected.

closest to Earth this year on 25 September. Discovered in 1781 by amateur astronomer William Herschel, Uranus was the first planet to be found since antiquity. Then, it doubled the size of our Solar System. Uranus is a gas giant like Jupiter, Saturn and Neptune. Four times the diameter of the Earth, it has an odd claim to fame: it orbits the Sun on its side (probably as a result of a collision in its infancy, which knocked it off its perch). Like the other gas giants, it has an encircling system of rings. But these are nothing like the spectacular edifices that girdle Saturn: the 11 rings are thin and faint. It also has a large family of moons – at the last count, 27. Many of us were disappointed when the Voyager probe flew past Uranus in 1986 to reveal a bland, featureless world. But things are hotting up as the planet's seasons change. Streaks and clouds are appearing in its atmosphere.

## SEPTEMBER'S PICTURE

The haunting wraiths of the **Veil Nebula** in **Cygnus** are the remains of a star that exploded over 5000 years ago. The twisted filaments are part of the Cygnus Loop – a reservoir of material swept up by the dead star that is expanding into space. One day, a phoenix will rise from the ashes: the gas will create a new generation of stars and planets – and, possibly, life.

## SEPTEMBER'S TOPIC
### The Harvest Moon

It's the time of year when farmers work late into the night, bringing home their ripe crops before autumn sets in. And traditionally they are aided by the light of the 'Harvest Moon' – a huge glowing Full Moon that seems to hang constant in the evening sky, rising at almost the same time night after night. At first sight, that doesn't seem possible. After all, the Moon is moving around the Earth, once in just under a month, so it ought to rise roughly one hour later every night. But things in the sky are hardly ever that simple....

The Moon follows a tilted path around the sky (close to the line of the Ecliptic, which is marked on the chart). And this path changes its angle with the horizon at different times of the year. On September evenings, the Moon's path runs roughly parallel to the horizon, so night after night the Moon moves to the left in the sky, but it hardly moves downwards. As a consequence, the Moon rises around the same time for several consecutive nights. This year, Full Moon on 12 September rises at 6.55 pm (ideal for harvesting) – it rises just 17 minutes earlier the evening before, and 17 minutes later the night after.

Jupiter is king of the night sky. To its right, you'll find the barren **Square of Pegasus** riding high in the south, joined by the faint and undistinguished constellations of autumn.

## OCTOBER'S CONSTELLATION

It takes considerable imagination to see the line of stars making up **Andromeda** as a young princess chained to a rock, about to be gobbled up by a vast sea monster (**Cetus**) – but that's ancient legends for you. Despite its rather mundane appearance, the constellation contains some surprising delights. One is **Almach**, the star at the left-hand end of the line. It's a beautiful double star. The main star is a yellow supergiant shining 650 times brighter than the Sun, and its companion – which is 5th magnitude – is bluish. The two stars are a lovely sight in small telescopes. Almach is actually a quadruple star: its companion is in fact triple.

But the glory of Andromeda is its great galaxy, beautifully placed on October nights. Lying above the line of stars, the **Andromeda Galaxy** (see Picture) is the most distant object easily visible to the unaided eye. It lies a mind-boggling 2.5 million light years away, yet it's so vast that it appears nearly four times as big as the Full Moon in the sky (although the sky will seldom be clear enough to allow you to see the faint outer regions).

The Andromeda Galaxy is the biggest member of the Local Group – it's estimated to contain over 400 billion stars. It is a wonderful sight in binoculars or a small telescope, and the latter will reveal its two bright companion galaxies – M32 and NGC205.

## PLANETS ON VIEW

Giant planet **Jupiter** is the undoubted 'star' of the month (see Object)! It's at opposition on 29 October, when it's opposite to the Sun in our skies and at its closest to Earth this

▼ *The sky at 11 pm in mid-October, with Moon positions at three-day intervals either side of Full Moon. The star positions are also correct for midnight at*

WEST

OPHIUCHUS
AQUILA
CORONA BOREALIS
HERCULES
LYRA
THE MILKY WAY
CYGNUS
Vega
BOÖTES
DRACO
Deneb
CANES VENATICI
The Plough
CEPHEUS
Zenith
CASSIOPEIA
Almach
URSA MINOR
Polaris
PERSEUS
NORTH
URSA MAJOR
Capella
AURIGA
15 Oct
Castor
GEMINI
Radiant of Orionids
Aldebaran
NE
Pollux
18 Oct
Betelgeuse
Ecliptic
ORION

EAST

*the beginning of October, and 9 pm at the end of the month (after the end of BST). The planets move slightly relative to the stars during the month.*

year. This enormous world is visible in the southern sky all night long, at magnitude −2.8, totally outshining the surrounding stars of Aries. A small telescope shows Jupiter's flattened globe, with multicoloured bands of cloud, while even binoculars will reveal the perpetual dance of its four biggest moons.

Meanwhile, competition is beginning to emerge as **Venus** (magnitude −3.8) begins to make its presence felt in the evening sky. By the end of October – while still in the twilight glow – the Evening Star is setting in the south-west almost an hour after the Sun.

**Mars**, at magnitude +1.2, rises in the north-east around 1 am. It starts the month in Praesepe (see Special Events). During October the Red Planet moves from Cancer to Leo.

Telescopic **Neptune** (magnitude +7.9) lies on the borders of Capricornus and Aquarius. The most distant planet sets around 2.30 am. **Uranus**, at magnitude +5.7, is in Pisces and sets about 5.30 am.

**Mercury** and **Saturn** are lost in the Sun's glare in October.

### MOON

On 1 October, the crescent Moon lies just above Antares. The Moon passes Jupiter on 13 October. In the morning of 22 October, you'll find the crescent Moon below Mars, with Regulus to its left.

### SPECIAL EVENTS

In the early hours of **1** and **2 October**, you'll find Mars right in front of Praesepe, the star cluster in

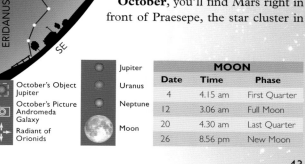

| | Jupiter |
| --- | --- |
| | Uranus |
| October's Object<br>Jupiter | Neptune |
| October's Picture<br>Andromeda<br>Galaxy | |
| Radiant of<br>Orionids | Moon |

| MOON | | |
| --- | --- | --- |
| **Date** | **Time** | **Phase** |
| 4 | 4.15 am | First Quarter |
| 12 | 3.06 am | Full Moon |
| 20 | 4.30 am | Last Quarter |
| 26 | 8.56 pm | New Moon |

Cancer known as the Beehive – a lovely sight in binoculars or a small telescope.

Debris from Halley's Comet smashes into Earth's atmosphere on **21/22 October**, causing the annual **Orionid** meteor shower.

At 2 am on **30 October**, we see the end of British Summer Time for this year. Clocks go backwards by an hour.

### OCTOBER'S OBJECT

**Jupiter** is particularly bright this month. On 29 October, it's at opposition – meaning that it's opposite the Sun in the sky, and at its closest to the Earth. 'Close' is a relative term, however – the planet is still over 590 million kilometres away. But Jupiter is so vast (at 143,000 kilometres in diameter, it could contain 1300 Earths) and as it's made almost entirely of gas, it's very efficient at reflecting sunlight.

Although Jupiter is so huge, it spins faster than any other planet in the Solar System. It rotates every 9 hours 55 minutes, and as a result its equator bulges outwards – through a small telescope, it looks a bit like a tangerine crossed with an old-

🔘 *Viewing tip*

Around 2.5 million light years away from us, the Andromeda Galaxy is often described as the furthest object easily visible to the unaided eye. But it's not that easy to see – especially if you are suffering some light pollution. The trick is to memorize the star patterns in Andromeda and look slightly to the side of where you expect the galaxy to be. This technique – called 'averted vision' – causes the image to fall on parts of the retina that are more light-sensitive than the central region, which is designed to see fine detail.

fashioned humbug. The humbug stripes are cloud belts of ammonia and methane stretched out by the planet's dizzy spin.

Jupiter has a fearsome magnetic field that no astronaut would survive, huge lightning storms, and an internal heat source which means it radiates more energy than it receives from the Sun. Jupiter's core simmers at a temperature of 20,000°C.

Jupiter commands its own 'mini-solar system' – a family of over 60 moons. The four biggest are visible in good binoculars, and even – to the really sharp-sighted – to the unaided eye. These are worlds in their own right (Ganymede is even larger than the planet Mercury). But two vie for 'star' status: Io and Europa. The surface of Io has incredible geysers erupting plumes of sulphur dioxide 300 kilometres into space. Brilliant white Europa probably contains oceans of liquid water beneath a solid ice crust, where alien fish may swim....

## OCTOBER'S PICTURE

The **Andromeda Galaxy** is one of the biggest spiral galaxies known, containing more stars than the Milky Way. Alas, it is presented to us at such a shallow angle that even the best photographs can't show the true glory of spiral arms. In this image, its companion galaxies – M32 (top) and NGC 205 (bottom) – flank their giant host.

## OCTOBER'S TOPIC
### Mars missions

America, Russia and China are all hoping to blast off to Mars this month. NASA is planning to launch its planetary rover Curiosity to the Red Planet. Ten times heavier than the current rovers on the Martian surface, this awesome beast will scoop up the planet's soil, and determine if it was – or, today, is – capable of harbouring microbial lifeforms.

Meanwhile, the Russians are busying themselves with the wonderfully named Phobos Grunt, aimed at Phobos – the Red Planet's major moon. Piggy-backing on board will be the Chinese Yinghuo-1 orbiting space probe. The two will part on arrival at Mars.

Phobos Grunt means 'Phobos soil'. And that's exactly what the spacecraft is designed to investigate. It will dig up a soil sample from Phobos – an irregularly-shaped moon less than 30 kilometres across – and send it back to Earth in 2012. Its composition will tell researchers how the Martian system came into being. It may also answer the question as to whether Phobos is a genuine moon of the Red Planet – or a planetoid that Mars has snatched from the nearby asteroid belt.

◀ *The Andromeda Galaxy, M31, photographed by Ian King using a 75 mm Pentax refractor and Starlight Xpress SXV-M25 CCD camera. He used separate exposures through individual colour filters.*

'A swarm of fireflies tangled in a silver braid' was the evocative description of the **Pleiades** star cluster by Alfred, Lord Tennyson, in his 1842 poem 'Locksley Hall'. All over the world, people have been intrigued by this lovely sight. From Greece to Australia, ancient myths independently describe the stars as a group of young girls being chased by an aggressive male – often **Aldebaran** or **Orion** – giving rise to the cluster's popular name, the Seven Sisters. Polynesian navigators used the Pleiades to mark the start of their year. And farmers in the Andes rely on the visibility of the Pleiades as a guide to planting their potatoes: the brightness or faintness of the Seven Sisters depends on El Niño, which affects the forthcoming weather. But once you see the Pleiades, you know that winter is here.

## NOVEMBER'S CONSTELLATION

It has to be said that **Pegasus** is one of the most boring constellations in the sky. A large, barren square of four medium-bright stars – how did our ancestors manage to see the shape of an upside-down winged horse up there?

In legend, Pegasus sprang from the blood of Medusa the Gorgon when **Perseus** (nearby in the sky) severed her head. But all pre-classical civilizations have their fabled winged horse, and we see them depicted on Etruscan and Euphratean vases.

The star at the top right of the square – **Scheat** – is a red giant over a hundred times wider than the Sun. Close to the end of its life, it pulsates irregularly, changing in brightness by about a magnitude. **Enif** ('the nose') – outside the square to the lower right – is a yellow supergiant. A small telescope, or even good binoculars, will reveal a faint blue companion star.

Just next to Enif – and Pegasus' best-kept secret – is the beautiful globular cluster **M15**. You'll need a telescope for this

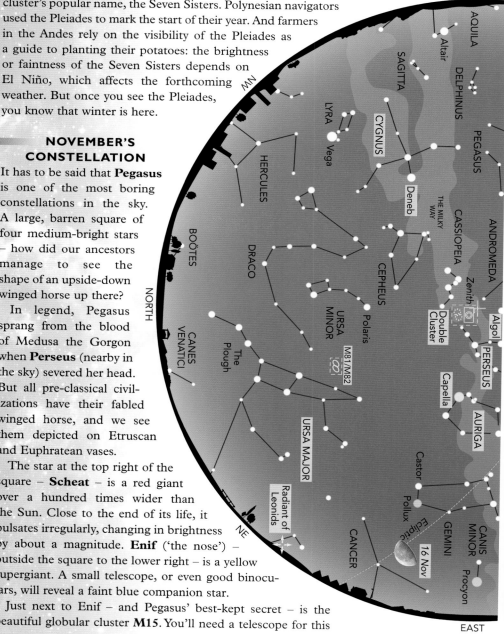

▼ The sky at 10 pm in mid-November, with Moon positions at three-day intervals either side of Full Moon. The star positions are also correct for 11 pm at

*the beginning of November, and 9 pm at the end of the month. The planets move slightly relative to the stars during the month.*

one. M15 is around 50,000 light years away, and contains about 200,000 stars.

## PLANETS ON VIEW

There's action low in the west after sunset, as **Venus** moves rapidly upwards. By the end of November, you'll find the Evening Star blazing at magnitude −3.8 in the south-west, and setting one-and-a-half hours after the Sun.

From 10 to 15 November, you may just catch **Mercury** (magnitude −0.1) lying below Venus. (It reaches greatest elongation on 14 November.) Because of the twilight glow, the innermost planet is best seen in binoculars.

Once Venus has set, **Jupiter** reigns supreme, at magnitude −2.7, on the borders of Aries and Pisces. The giant planet sets around 5.30 am.

At magnitude +7.9, a small telescope shows **Neptune** in Aquarius, setting around 11.30 pm. Binoculars will suffice to reveal **Uranus** (magnitude +5.7): lying in Pisces, the dim green planet sets at about 2.30 am.

**Mars** brightens from magnitude +1.1 to +0.7 during November, as the Earth catches up with the slower planet. Rising about 11.30 pm, the Red Planet lies in Leo. It passes the lion's brightest star, Regulus, on 9 November: compare the ochre colour of Mars with the blue-white star.

And just before dawn, you can spot **Saturn** returning from its sojourn behind the Sun. The ringed planet is rising around 4.30 am, in

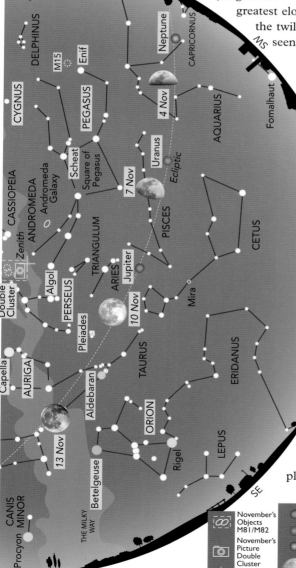

WEST

EAST

| | | November's Objects M81/M82 |
| November's Picture Double Cluster |
| Radiant of Leonids |

| | | Jupiter |
| | | Uranus |
| | | Neptune |
| | | Moon |

| MOON | | |
|------|------|-------|
| Date | Time | Phase |
| 2 | 4.38 pm | First Quarter |
| 10 | 8.16 pm | Full Moon |
| 18 | 3.09 pm | Last Quarter |
| 25 | 6.10 am | New Moon |

Virgo. At magnitude +1.0 it's a close twin to the constellation's brightest star, Spica, which lies just below Saturn.

## MOON

You'll find the Moon, almost Full, near Jupiter on 9 November. On the morning of 19 November, the waning Moon lies below Mars and Regulus. And the mornings of 22 and 23 November see the crescent Moon near Saturn and Spica. Back in the evening sky, the waxing crescent Moon forms a lovely duo with Venus on 26 and 27 November.

## SPECIAL EVENTS

The night of **17/18 November** sees the maximum of the **Leonid** meteor shower. A few years ago, this annual shower yielded literally storms of shooting stars, but the rate has gone down as the parent Comet Tempel-Tuttle, which sheds its dust to produce the meteors, has moved away from the vicinity of Earth.

There's a partial eclipse of the Sun on **25 November**, but it's only visible from Antarctica and parts of the Southern Ocean.

## NOVEMBER'S OBJECT

A pair of galaxies this month, in **Ursa Major**, called **M81** and **M82**. You can just see each of these galaxies with binoculars, on a really dark night, though a moderately powerful telescope is needed to reveal them in detail. 'M', incidentally, stands for Charles Messier, an 18th-century Parisian astronomer who catalogued 103 'fuzzy objects' that misleadingly resembled comets, which he was desperate to discover. He did find a handful of comets – but today, he's better remembered for his Messier Catalogue.

M81 is a beautiful, smooth spiral galaxy, like our Milky Way, with spiral arms wrapped around a softly-glowing core. It's similar in size and mass to our own Galaxy, and lies 11 million light years away.

Lying close by is M82 – another spiral galaxy, but one which couldn't be more different. It looks a total mess, with a huge eruption taking place at its core. This is a result of an interaction with M81 some 300 million years

▼ *The Double Cluster in Perseus, NGC 869 (right) and NGC 884, photographed by Peter Shah through a 200 mm Orion Optics AG8 reflector with Starlight Xpress CCD camera, with four separate 10-minute exposures – one each through red, green and blue filters, and an unfiltered exposure.*

### Viewing tip

Now that the nights are drawing in earlier, and becoming darker, it's a good time to pick out faint, fuzzy objects like the Andromeda Galaxy and the Orion Nebula. But don't even think about it near the time of Full Moon – its light will drown them out. The best time to observe 'deep-sky objects' is when the Moon is near to New, or well after Full Moon. Check the Moon phases timetable in the book.

ago, when the two galaxies pulled streams of interstellar gas out of one another. Gas clouds are still raining on to M82's core, creating an explosion of star formation. For this reason, M82 is called a 'starburst' galaxy.

## NOVEMBER'S PICTURE

This beautiful pair of star clusters in **Perseus** – the **Double Cluster** – is a glorious sight in binoculars. Medium-sized telescopes reveal that each cluster contains about 300 stars, but this is only the tip of the iceberg: there are probably thousands of stars in residence. The stars are very young (in astronomical terms!) – between 3 million and 5 million years old, as compared to our Sun's 5000 million years.

## NOVEMBER'S TOPIC
### Star names

Why do the brightest stars have such strange names? The reason is that they date from antiquity, and have been passed on down generations ever since. The original western star names – like the original constellations – were probably Babylonian or Chaldean, but few of these survive. The Greeks took up the baton after that, and the name of the star **Antares** is a direct result. It means 'rival of Ares' because its red colour rivals that of the planet Mars (*Ares* in Greek).

The Romans were not particularly interested in astronomy, but nevertheless left their mark on the sky. **Capella**, the brightest star of **Auriga**, has Roman roots: the name is a diminutive of *capra* (goat), and it literally means 'the little she-goat' (a bit of an understatement for a star over 100 times brighter than the Sun).

But the Arabs were largely responsible for the star names we have inherited today. Working in the so-called 'Dark Ages' between the 6th and 10th centuries AD, they took over the naming of the sky – hence the number of stars beginning with the letters 'al' (Arabic for 'the'). **Algol**, in the constellation **Perseus**, means 'the demon' – possibly because the Arabs noticed that its brightness seems to 'wink' every few days. **Deneb**, in **Cygnus**, also has Arabic roots – it means 'the tail' (of the flying bird).

But the most remembered star name in the sky is Orion's **Betelgeuse**. For some time, it was gloriously interpreted as 'the armpit of the sacred one'. But the 'B' in Betelgeuse turned out to be a mistransliteration – and so we're none the wiser as to how our distant ancestors really identified this fiery red star.

This year, we have a Christmas Star: the planet Venus, shining brilliantly in the sunset at twilight. But it's the nadir of the year – December sees the shortest day, and the longest night, when Earth's North Pole is turned away from our local star. On 22 December, we hit the Winter Solstice. It has long been commemorated in tablets of stone, aligned to welcome the returning Sun.

▼ The sky at 10 pm in mid-December, with Moon positions at three-day intervals either side of Full Moon. The star positions are also correct for 11 pm at

## DECEMBER'S CONSTELLATION

**Taurus** is very much a second cousin to brilliant **Orion**, but a fascinating constellation nonetheless. It's dominated by **Aldebaran**, the baleful blood-red eye of the celestial bull. Around 68 light years away, and shining with a magnitude of +0.85, Aldebaran is a red giant star, but not one as extreme as neighbouring **Betelgeuse**. It is around three times heavier than the Sun. The 'head' of the bull is formed by the **Hyades** star cluster. The other famous star cluster in Taurus is the far more glamorous **Pleiades**, whose stars – although further away than the Hyades – are younger and brighter.

Taurus has two 'horns' – the star **El Nath** (Arabic for 'the butting one') to the north, and **zeta Tauri** (whose Babylonian name Shurnarkabti-sha-shutu, meaning 'star in the bull towards the south', is thankfully not generally used!). Above this star is a stellar wreck – literally. In 1054, Chinese astronomers witnessed a brilliant 'new star' appear in this spot, which was visible in daytime for weeks. What the Chinese actually saw was an exploding star – a supernova – in its death throes. And today, we see its still-expanding remains as the **Crab Nebula**. It's visible through a medium-sized telescope.

*the beginning of December, and 9 pm at the end of the month. The planets move slightly relative to the stars during the month.*

## PLANETS ON VIEW

**Venus** is the Christmas Star of 2011. The Evening Star hangs like a lantern in the south-west after sunset, at magnitude −3.9. By New Year's Eve, it's setting three hours after the Sun and is visible in a dark sky for the first time since January.

Venus's brilliance has knocked **Jupiter** from its dominance. You can find the giant planet at 'only' magnitude −2.5 (still brighter than any star) on the borders of Aries and Pisces, and setting around 3.15 am.

Faint **Neptune** (magnitude +7.9), in Aquarius, is setting around 9.30 pm. It's followed by slightly brighter twin **Uranus** (magnitude +5.8), lying in Pisces and dropping below the horizon about 0.30 am.

After months hiding itself away until the early hours, **Mars** is now part of the evening scene, rising in the east about 10.45 pm (just too late for our chart). During the month, the Red Planet tracks along under the belly of Leo, and brightens from magnitude +0.7 to +0.2.

**Saturn** rises around 2.40 am, shining at magnitude +1.0 in Virgo, to the left of Spica.

Finally, in the second part of the month you may catch **Mercury** (magnitude 0.0) in the dawn twilight; it's at greatest western elongation on 23 December. Look low in the south-east around 6.30 am, between 12 and 31 December.

## MOON

On 6 December, the Moon lies immediately above Jupiter. On the night of

| MOON | | |
|---|---|---|
| **Date** | **Time** | **Phase** |
| 2 | 9.52 am | First Quarter |
| 10 | 2.37 pm | Full Moon |
| 18 | 0.47 am | Last Quarter |
| 24 | 6.06 pm | New Moon |

WEST

WEST

AQUARIUS

1 Dec

PEGASUS

Square of Pegasus

Uranus

4 Dec

Ecliptic

PISCES

Uranus

CETUS

ANDROMEDA

TRIANGULUM

Jupiter

ARIES

Mira

Zenith

Algol

PERSEUS

7 Dec

Capella

Pleiades

Hyades

TAURUS

ERIDANUS

SOUTH

AURIGA

10 Dec

El Nath

zeta

Aldebaran

Rigel

Radiant of Geminids

GEMINI

Crab Nebula

Betelgeuse

Horsehead Nebula

ORION

LEPUS

COLUMBA

Castor

Pollux

13 Dec

Procyon

CANIS MINOR

THE MILKY WAY

Sirius

CANIS MAJOR

Adhara

SE

CANCER

HYDRA

EAST

December's Object Algol

December's Picture Horsehead Nebula

Radiant of Geminids

Jupiter

Uranus

Moon

51

10/11 December, the Full Moon moves directly in front of the Crab Nebula (see Special Events). The Moon passes below Regulus on 15 December, and it's near Mars on 16 and 17 December. On the morning of 20 December, the crescent Moon lies below Saturn and Spica. The dawn skies of 22 and 23 December see the narrow crescent near to Mercury. On the evenings of 26 and 27 December, there's a lovely pairing of the waxing crescent and Venus.

▶ Peter Shah took this view of the Horsehead Nebula in Orion using his 200 mm Newtonian reflector and CCD. He gave a total exposure time of 2 hours 50 minutes through separate red, green, blue and hydrogen alpha filters from his home in Meifod, Wales. North is at the left.

## SPECIAL EVENTS

The maximum of the **Geminid** meteor shower falls on **13/14 December**. These shooting stars are debris shed from an asteroid called Phaethon and therefore quite substantial – and hence bright. But this year the show will be spoilt by moonlight.

There's a total eclipse of the Moon on **10 December**, but it will be a damp squib as seen from the UK. The total phase is over by the time the Moon rises in the north-east at 4.00 pm, and the partial eclipse finishes by 4.15 pm.

On the night of **10/11 December** (between 2.30 and 3.30 am), the Moon occults the Crab Nebula. Even with a telescope, this unusual event will be a challenge, as the Moon will be just past Full, and at its brightest.

The Winter Solstice occurs at 5.30 am on **22 December**. As a result of the tilt of Earth's axis, the Sun reaches its lowest point in the heavens as seen from the northern hemisphere: we get the shortest days, and the longest nights.

## DECEMBER'S OBJECT

The star **Algol**, in the constellation **Perseus**, represents the head of the dreadful Gorgon Medusa. In Arabic, its name means 'the demon'. Watch Algol carefully and you'll see why. Every 2 days 21 hours, Algol dims in brightness for several hours – to become as faint as the star lying to its lower right (Gorgonea Tertia).

In 1783, a young British amateur astronomer, John Goodricke of York, discovered Algol's regular changes, and proposed that Algol is orbited by a large dark planet that periodically blocks off some of its light. We now know that Algol does indeed have a dim companion blocking its brilliant light, but it's a fainter star rather than a planet.

## DECEMBER'S PICTURE

One of the most iconic of astronomical tourist spots, the **Horsehead Nebula** is part of the huge star-forming region in the constellation of **Orion**. This celestial chess-piece measures 4 light years from 'nose' to 'mane'. It's a dark cloud of cosmic soot, which will collapse under gravity to form a new generation of stars.

### ◉ Viewing tip

This is the month when you may be thinking of buying a telescope as a Christmas present for a budding stargazer. Beware! Unscrupulous mail-order catalogues selling 'gadgets' often advertise small telescopes that boast huge magnifications. This is known as 'empty magnification' – blowing up an image that the lens or mirror simply doesn't have the ability to get to grips with, so all you see is a bigger blur. A rule of thumb is to use a maximum magnification no greater than twice the diameter of your lens or mirror in millimetres. So if you have a 100 mm reflecting telescope, go no higher than 200X.

## DECEMBER'S TOPIC
### Search for Extra-Terrestrial Intelligence

Whenever we give a presentation, one of the questions we're most asked is: 'Is there anybody out there?' It's now half a century since the veteran American astronomer Frank Drake turned his radio telescope to the heavens in the hope of hearing an alien broadcast. Despite false alarms (probably caused by secret military equipment), there has been a deafening silence.

Drake and his colleagues founded an independent institution in California – the SETI Institute (Search for Extra-Terrestrial Intelligence). It's a serious scientific endeavour that looks into the biology, psychology and motivation for our search for alien life.

Recently, their fortunes have been boosted by a donation from Paul Allen (who co-founded Microsoft). Thanks to Allen, the team is now building an array of 400 radio telescopes in California to tune in to that first whisper from ET.

But is life out there far more advanced than us? Is radio communication something that came and went? The SETI researchers are contemplating communicating with laser beams – but even that may prove too primitive.

There's always something to see in our Solar System, from planets to meteors or the Moon. These objects are very close to us – in astronomical terms – so their positions, shapes and sizes appear to change constantly. It is important to know when, where and how to look if you are to enjoy exploring Earth's neighbourhood. Here we give the best dates in 2011 for observing the planets and meteors (weather permitting!), and explain some of the concepts that will help you to get the most out of your observing.

### THE INFERIOR PLANETS

A planet with an orbit that lies closer to the Sun than the orbit of Earth is known as *inferior*. Mercury and Venus are the inferior planets. They show a full range of phases (like the Moon) from the thinnest crescents to full, depending on their position in relation to the Earth and the Sun. The diagram below shows the various positions of the inferior planets. They are invisible when at *conjunction*, when they are either behind the Sun, or between the Earth and the Sun, and lost in the latter's glare.

**Magnitudes**

Astronomers measure the brightness of stars, planets and other celestial objects using a scale of *magnitudes*. Somewhat confusingly, fainter objects have higher magnitudes, while brighter objects have lower magnitudes; the most brilliant stars have negative magnitudes! Naked-eye stars range from magnitude −1.5 for the brightest star, Sirius, to +6.5 for the faintest stars you can see on a really dark night.

As a guide, here are the magnitudes of selected objects:

| | |
|---|---|
| Sun | −26.7 |
| Full Moon | −12.5 |
| Venus (at its brightest) | −4.7 |
| Sirius | −1.5 |
| Betelgeuse | +0.4 |
| Polaris (Pole Star) | +2.0 |
| Faintest star visible to the naked eye | +6.5 |
| Faintest star visible to the Hubble Space Telescope | +31 |

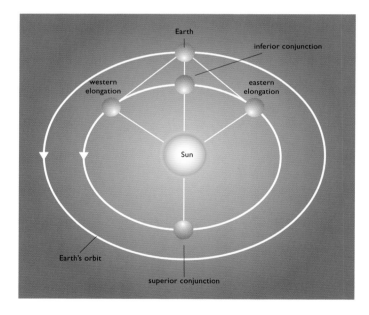

◄ At eastern or western elongation, an inferior planet is at its maximum angular distance from the Sun. Conjunction occurs at two stages in the planet's orbit. Under certain circumstances, an inferior planet can transit across the Sun's disc at inferior conjunction.

### Mercury

In the first few weeks of January, Mercury is visible low in the south-east before dawn; it reaches its greatest western elongation on 9 January. It re-emerges in the second half of March for its best evening appearance of the year, but disappears again in April. Its best morning appearances are in early September and mid–late December.

| ◯ Maximum elongations of Mercury in 2011 | |
|---|---|
| Date | Separation |
| 9 January | 23.3° west |
| 23 March | 18.6° east |
| 7 May | 26.6° west |
| 20 July | 26.8° east |
| 3 September | 18.1° west |
| 14 November | 22.7° east |
| 23 December | 21.8° west |

| Maximum elongation of Venus in 2011 | |
|---|---|
| Date | Separation |
| 8 January | 47.0° west |

## Venus

Venus reaches its greatest western elongation of 2011 on 8 January. From the beginning of the year onwards it is brilliant in the east as a Morning Star, hugging the horizon, but disappears from view by August. It re-emerges as an Evening Star towards the end of October.

### THE SUPERIOR PLANETS

The superior planets are those with orbits that lie beyond that of the Earth. They are Mars, Jupiter, Saturn, Uranus and Neptune. The best time to observe a superior planet is when the Earth lies between it and the Sun. At this point in a planet's orbit, it is said to be at *opposition*.

▶ *Superior planets are invisible at conjunction. At quadrature the planet is at right angles to the Sun as viewed from Earth. Opposition is the best time to observe a superior planet.*

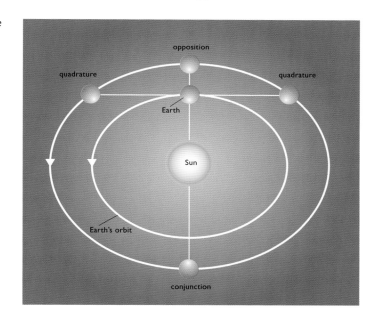

| Progress of Mars through the constellations | |
|---|---|
| Late June – end July | Taurus |
| August – mid-Sept | Gemini |
| Mid-Sept – mid-Oct | Cancer |
| Mid-Oct – end Dec | Leo |

## Mars

Mars is lost from view at the start of the year, and only emerges from the Sun's glare in the last week of June. The Red Planet is at its best during the second half of the year, reaching its brightest magnitude of 2011 in December.

## Jupiter

Jupiter is visible in the west from January onwards, in Pisces, but by the end of March it has already disappeared into the twilight glow. It starts to reappear in the east at the very end of May. Moving into Aries, Jupiter brightens each month until its best showing in October, when it is visible in the southern sky all night long. It reaches opposition on 29 October.

### Saturn

Saturn is in Virgo all year. It is at opposition on 3 April, and is at its best for observing from January to July. It is lost from view by the end of August, but re-emerges in the morning during November.

### Uranus

Uranus is best viewed in early January, when it lies in Pisces, but by the end of February it has disappeared into the twilight glow. It reappears in June, and visibility improves into the autumn. Uranus reaches opposition on 25 September.

### Neptune

Neptune is best viewed from May onwards, when it lies in Aquarius. It is at opposition on 22 August.

## SOLAR AND LUNAR ECLIPSES

### Solar Eclipses

There are four partial solar eclipses in 2011. The first, on 4 January, can be seen from south-east England. However, the second partial eclipse, on 1 June, will only be viewable from around the Arctic Ocean. The third partial eclipse, on 1 July, can be seen only from near Antarctica; similarly, the fourth partial eclipse of the year, on 25 November, will only be viewable from Antarctica and parts of the Southern Ocean.

### Lunar Eclipses

The lunar eclipse on 15 June will be total as seen from the UK, but unfortunately not in a dark sky, so it will not be visible after all. The total lunar eclipse on 10 December will also be a disappointment for UK observers, as the total phase is over by the time the Moon rises in the north-east.

**Astronomical distances**

For objects in the Solar System, such as the planets, we can give their distances from the Earth in kilometres. But the distances are just too huge once we reach out to the stars. Even the nearest star (Proxima Centauri) lies 25 million million kilometres away.

So astronomers use a larger unit – the *light year*. This is the distance that light travels in one year, and it equals 9.46 million million kilometres.

Here are the distances to some familiar astronomical objects, in light years:

| | |
|---|---|
| Proxima Centauri | 4.2 |
| Betelgeuse | 600 |
| Centre of the Milky Way | 26,000 |
| Andromeda Galaxy | 2.5 million |
| Most distant galaxies seen by the Hubble Space Telescope | 13 billion |

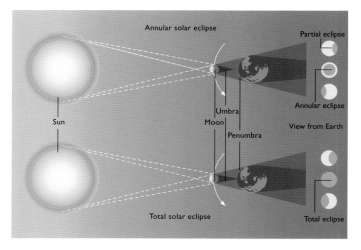

*Annular solar eclipse*

*Partial eclipse*

*Umbra*

*Moon*

*Annular eclipse*

*Penumbra*

*View from Earth*

*Sun*

*Total solar eclipse*

*Total eclipse*

◀ *Where the dark central part (the umbra) of the Moon's shadow reaches the Earth, we see a total eclipse. People located within the penumbra see a partial eclipse. If the umbral shadow does not reach the Earth, we see an annular eclipse. This type of eclipse occurs when the Moon is at a distant point in its orbit and is not quite large enough to cover the whole of the Sun's disc.*

| Dates of maximum for selected meteor showers | |
|---|---|
| Meteor shower | Date of maximum |
| Quadrantids | 3/4 January |
| Lyrids | 22/23 April |
| Eta Aquarids | 4/5 May |
| Perseids | 12/13 August |
| Orionids | 21/22 October |
| Leonids | 17/18 November |
| Geminids | 13/14 December |

▶ *Meteors from a common source, occurring during a shower, enter the atmosphere along parallel trajectories. As a result of perspective, however, they appear to diverge from a single point in the sky – the radiant.*

## METEOR SHOWERS

Shooting stars – or *meteors* – are tiny particles of interplanetary dust, known as *meteoroids*, burning up in the Earth's atmosphere. At certain times of year, the Earth passes through a stream of these meteoroids (usually debris left behind by a comet) and we see a *meteor shower*. The point in the sky from which the meteors appear to emanate is known as the *radiant*. Most showers are known by the constellation in which the radiant is situated.

Observer's field of view

When watching meteors for a co-ordinated meteor programme, observers generally note the time, seeing conditions, cloud cover, their own location, the time and brightness of each meteor, and whether it was from the main meteor stream. It is also worth noting details of persistent afterglows (trains) and fireballs, and making counts of how many meteors appear in a given period.

**Angular separations**

Astronomers measure the distance between objects, as we see them in the sky, by the angle between the objects in degrees (symbol °). From the horizon to the point above your head is 90 degrees. All around the horizon is 360 degrees.

You can use your hand, held at arm's length, as a rough guide to angular distances, as follows:

Width of index finger 1°
Width of clenched hand 10°
Thumb to little finger
  on outspread hand 20°
For smaller distances, astronomers divide the degree into 60 arcminutes (symbol ′), and the arcminute into 60 arcseconds (symbol ″).

## COMETS

Comets are small bodies in orbit about the Sun. Consisting of frozen gases and dust, they are often known as 'dirty snowballs'. When their orbits bring them close to the Sun, the ices evaporate and dramatic tails of gas and dust can sometimes be seen.

A number of comets move round the Sun in fairly small, elliptical orbits in periods of a few years; others have much longer periods. Most really brilliant comets have orbital periods of several thousands or even millions of years. The exception is Comet Halley, a bright comet with a period of about 76 years. It was last seen with the naked eye in 1986.

Binoculars and wide-field telescopes provide the best views of comet tails. Larger telescopes with a high magnification are necessary to observe fine detail in the gaseous head (*coma*). Most comets are discovered with professional instruments, but a few are still found by experienced amateur astronomers.

None of the known comets is predicted to reach naked-eye brightness in 2011, but there's always a chance of a bright new comet putting in a surprise appearance.

Deep-sky objects are 'fuzzy patches' that lie outside the Solar System. They include star clusters, nebulae and galaxies. To observe the majority of deep-sky objects you will need binoculars or a telescope, but there are also some beautiful naked-eye objects, notably the Pleiades and the Orion Nebula.

The faintest object that an instrument can see is its *limiting magnitude*. The table gives a rough guide, for good seeing conditions, for a variety of small- to medium-sized telescopes.

We have provided a selection of recommended deep-sky targets, together with their magnitudes. Some are described in more detail in our monthly 'Object' features. Look on the appropriate month's map to find which constellations are on view, and then choose your objects using the list below. We have provided celestial coordinates for readers with detailed star maps. The suggested times of year for viewing are when the constellation is highest in the sky in the late evening.

| Limiting magnitude for small to medium telescopes | |
| --- | --- |
| Aperture (mm) | Limiting magnitude |
| 50 | +11.2 |
| 60 | +11.6 |
| 70 | +11.9 |
| 80 | +12.2 |
| 100 | +12.7 |
| 125 | +13.2 |
| 150 | +13.6 |

## RECOMMENDED DEEP-SKY OBJECTS

**Andromeda** – autumn and early winter

| M31 (NGC 224) Andromeda Galaxy | 3rd-magnitude spiral galaxy RA 00h 42.7m Dec +41° 16' |
| --- | --- |
| M32 (NGC 221) | 8th-magnitude elliptical galaxy, a companion to M31 RA 00h 42.7m Dec +40° 52' |
| M110 (NGC 205) | 8th-magnitude elliptical galaxy RA 00h 40.4m Dec +41° 41' |
| NGC 7662 Blue Snowball | 8th-magnitude planetary nebula RA 23h 25.9m Dec +42° 33' |

**Aquarius** – late autumn and early winter

| M2 (NGC 7089) | 6th-magnitude globular cluster RA 21h 33.5m Dec –00° 49' |
| --- | --- |
| M72 (NGC 6981) | 9th-magnitude globular cluster RA 20h 53.5m Dec –12° 32' |
| NGC 7293 Helix Nebula | 7th-magnitude planetary nebula RA 22h 29.6m Dec –20° 48' |
| NGC 7009 Saturn Nebula | 8th-magnitude planetary nebula RA 21h 04.2m Dec –11° 22' |

**Aries** – early winter

| NGC 772 | 10th-magnitude spiral galaxy RA 01h 59.3m Dec +19° 01' |
| --- | --- |

**Auriga** – winter

| M36 (NGC 1960) | 6th-magnitude open cluster RA 05h 36.1m Dec +34° 08' |
| --- | --- |
| M37 (NGC 2099) | 6th-magnitude open cluster RA 05h 52.4m Dec +32° 33' |
| M38 (NGC 1912) | 6th-magnitude open cluster RA 05h 28.7m Dec +35° 50' |

**Cancer** – late winter to early spring

| M44 (NGC 2632) Praesepe or Beehive | 3rd-magnitude open cluster RA 08h 40.1m Dec +19° 59' |
| --- | --- |
| M67 (NGC 2682) | 7th-magnitude open cluster RA 08h 50.4m Dec +11° 49' |

**Canes Venatici** – visible all year

| M3 (NGC 5272) | 6th-magnitude globular cluster RA 13h 42.2m Dec +28° 23' |
| --- | --- |

| M51 (NGC 5194/5) Whirlpool Galaxy | 8th-magnitude spiral galaxy RA 13h 29.9m Dec +47° 12' |
| --- | --- |
| M63 (NGC 5055) | 9th-magnitude spiral galaxy RA 13h 15.8m Dec +42° 02' |
| M94 (NGC 4736) | 8th-magnitude spiral galaxy RA 12h 50.9m Dec +41° 07' |
| M106 (NGC4258) | 8th-magnitude spiral galaxy RA 12h 19.0m Dec +47° 18' |

**Canis Major** – late winter

| M41 (NGC 2287) | 4th-magnitude open cluster RA 06h 47.0m Dec –20° 44' |
| --- | --- |

**Capricornus** – late summer and early autumn

| M30 (NGC 7099) | 7th-magnitude globular cluster RA 21h 40.4m Dec –23° 11' |
| --- | --- |

**Cassiopeia** – visible all year

| M52 (NGC 7654) | 6th-magnitude open cluster RA 23h 24.2m Dec +61° 35' |
| --- | --- |
| M103 (NGC 581) | 7th-magnitude open cluster RA 01h 33.2m Dec +60° 42' |
| NGC 225 | 7th-magnitude open cluster RA 00h 43.4m Dec +61 47' |
| NGC 457 | 6th-magnitude open cluster RA 01h 19.1m Dec +58° 20' |
| NGC 663 | Good binocular open cluster RA 01h 46.0m Dec +61° 15' |

**Cepheus** – visible all year

| Delta Cephei | Variable star, varying between +3.5 and +4.4 with a period of 5.37 days. It has a magnitude +6.3 companion and they make an attractive pair for small telescopes or binoculars. |
| --- | --- |

**Cetus** – late autumn

| Mira (omicron Ceti) | Irregular variable star with a period of roughly 330 days and a range between +2.0 and +10.1. |
| --- | --- |
| M77 (NGC 1068) | 9th-magnitude spiral galaxy RA 02h 42.7m Dec –00° 01' |

## Coma Berenices – spring

| | |
|---|---|
| M53 (NGC 5024) | 8th-magnitude globular cluster<br>*RA 13h 12.9m Dec +18° 10'* |
| M64 (NGC 4286)<br>Black Eye Galaxy | 8th-magnitude spiral galaxy with a prominent dust lane that is visible in larger telescopes.<br>*RA 12h 56.7m Dec +21° 41'* |
| M85 (NGC 4382) | 9th-magnitude elliptical galaxy<br>*RA 12h 25.4m Dec +18° 11'* |
| M88 (NGC 4501) | 10th-magnitude spiral galaxy<br>*RA 12h 32.0m Dec +14° 25'* |
| M91 (NGC 4548) | 10th-magnitude spiral galaxy<br>*RA 12h 35.4m Dec +14° 30'* |
| M98 (NGC 4192) | 10th-magnitude spiral galaxy<br>*RA 12h 13.8m Dec +14° 54'* |
| M99 (NGC 4254) | 10th-magnitude spiral galaxy<br>*RA 12h 18.8m Dec +14° 25'* |
| M100 (NGC 4321) | 9th-magnitude spiral galaxy<br>*RA 12h 22.9m Dec +15° 49'* |
| NGC 4565 | 10th-magnitude spiral galaxy<br>*RA 12h 36.3m Dec +25° 59'* |

## Cygnus – late summer and autumn

| | |
|---|---|
| Cygnus Rift | Dark cloud just south of Deneb that appears to split the Milky Way in two. |
| NGC 7000<br>North America Nebula | A bright nebula against the background of the Milky Way, visible with binoculars under dark skies.<br>*RA 20h 58.8m Dec +44° 20'* |
| NGC 6992<br>Veil Nebula (part) | Supernova remnant, visible with binoculars under dark skies.<br>*RA 20h 56.8m Dec +31 28'* |
| M29 (NGC 6913) | 7th-magnitude open cluster<br>*RA 20h 23.9m Dec +36° 32'* |
| M39 (NGC 7092) | Large 5th-magnitude open cluster<br>*RA 21h 32.2m Dec +48° 26'* |
| NGC 6826<br>Blinking Planetary | 9th-magnitude planetary nebula<br>*RA 19 44.8m Dec +50° 31'* |

## Delphinus – late summer

| | |
|---|---|
| NGC 6934 | 9th-magnitude globular cluster<br>*RA 20h 34.2m Dec +07° 24'* |

## Draco – midsummer

| | |
|---|---|
| NGC 6543 | 9th-magnitude planetary nebula<br>*RA 17h 58.6m Dec +66° 38'* |

## Gemini – winter

| | |
|---|---|
| M35 (NGC 2168) | 5th-magnitude open cluster<br>*RA 06h 08.9m Dec +24° 20'* |
| NGC 2392<br>Eskimo Nebula | 8–10th-magnitude planetary nebula<br>*RA 07h 29.2m Dec +20° 55'* |

## Hercules – early summer

| | |
|---|---|
| M13 (NGC 6205) | 6th-magnitude globular cluster<br>*RA 16h 41.7m Dec +36° 28'* |
| M92 (NGC 6341) | 6th-magnitude globular cluster<br>*RA 17h 17.1m Dec +43° 08'* |
| NGC 6210 | 9th-magnitude planetary nebula<br>*RA 16h 44.5m Dec +23 49'* |

## Hydra – early spring

| | |
|---|---|
| M48 (NGC 2548) | 6th-magnitude open cluster<br>*RA 08h 13.8m Dec –05° 48'* |
| M68 (NGC 4590) | 8th-magnitude globular cluster<br>*RA 12h 39.5m Dec –26° 45'* |

## M83 (NGC 5236)

| | |
|---|---|
| M83 (NGC 5236) | 8th-magnitude spiral galaxy<br>*RA 13h 37.0m Dec –29° 52'* |
| NGC 3242<br>Ghost of Jupiter | 9th-magnitude planetary nebula<br>*RA 10h 24.8m Dec –18°38'* |

## Leo – spring

| | |
|---|---|
| M65 (NGC 3623) | 9th-magnitude spiral galaxy<br>*RA 11h 18.9m Dec +13° 05'* |
| M66 (NGC 3627) | 9th-magnitude spiral galaxy<br>*RA 11h 20.2m Dec +12° 59'* |
| M95 (NGC 3351) | 10th-magnitude spiral galaxy<br>*RA 10h 44.0m Dec +11° 42'* |
| M96 (NGC 3368) | 9th-magnitude spiral galaxy<br>*RA 10h 46.8m Dec +11° 49'* |
| M105 (NGC 3379) | 9th-magnitude elliptical galaxy<br>*RA 10h 47.8m Dec +12° 35'* |

## Lepus – winter

| | |
|---|---|
| M79 (NGC 1904) | 8th-magnitude globular cluster<br>*RA 05h 24.5m Dec –24° 33'* |

## Lyra – spring

| | |
|---|---|
| M56 (NGC 6779) | 8th-magnitude globular cluster<br>*RA 19h 16.6m Dec +30° 11'* |
| M57 (NGC 6720)<br>Ring Nebula | 9th-magnitude planetary nebula<br>*RA 18h 53.6m Dec +33° 02'* |

## Monoceros – winter

| | |
|---|---|
| M50 (NGC 2323) | 6th-magnitude open cluster<br>*RA 07h 03.2m Dec –08° 20'* |
| NGC 2244 | Open cluster surrounded by the faint Rosette Nebula, NGC 2237. Visible in binoculars.<br>*RA 06h 32.4m Dec +04° 52'* |

## Ophiuchus – summer

| | |
|---|---|
| M9 (NGC 6333) | 8th-magnitude globular cluster<br>*RA 17h 19.2m Dec –18° 31'* |
| M10 (NGC 6254) | 7th-magnitude globular cluster<br>*RA 16h 57.1m Dec –04° 06'* |
| M12 (NCG 6218) | 7th-magnitude globular cluster<br>*RA 16h 47.2m Dec –01° 57'* |
| M14 (NGC 6402) | 8th-magnitude globular cluster<br>*RA 17h 37.6m Dec –03° 15'* |
| M19 (NGC 6273) | 7th-magnitude globular cluster<br>*RA 17h 02.6m Dec –26° 16'* |
| M62 (NGC 6266) | 7th-magnitude globular cluster<br>*RA 17h 01.2m Dec –30° 07'* |
| M107 (NGC 6171) | 8th-magnitude globular cluster<br>*RA 16h 32.5m Dec –13° 03'* |

## Orion – winter

| | |
|---|---|
| M42 (NGC 1976)<br>Orion Nebula | 4th-magnitude nebula<br>*RA 05h 35.4m Dec –05° 27'* |
| M43 (NGC 1982) | 5th-magnitude nebula<br>*RA 05h 35.6m Dec –05° 16'* |
| M78 (NGC 2068) | 8th-magnitude nebula<br>*RA 05h 46.7m Dec +00° 03'* |

## Pegasus – autumn

| | |
|---|---|
| M15 (NGC 7078) | 6th-magnitude globular cluster<br>*RA 21h 30.0m Dec +12° 10'* |

## Perseus – autumn to winter

| | |
|---|---|
| M34 (NGC 1039) | 5th-magnitude open cluster<br>*RA 02h 42.0m Dec +42° 47'* |
| M76 (NGC 650/1)<br>Little Dumbbell | 11th-magnitude planetary nebula<br>*RA 01h 42.4m Dec +51° 34'* |

| NGC 869/884 | Pair of open star clusters |
|---|---|
| Double Cluster | RA 02h 19.0m Dec +57° 09' |
| | RA 02h 22.4m Dec +57° 07' |

**Pisces** – autumn

| M74 (NGC 628) | 9th-magnitude spiral galaxy |
|---|---|
| | RA 01h 36.7m Dec +15° 47' |

**Puppis** – late winter

| M46 (NGC 2437) | 6th-magnitude open cluster |
|---|---|
| | RA 07h 41.8m Dec –14° 49' |
| M47 (NGC 2422) | 4th-magnitude open cluster |
| | RA 07h 36.6m Dec –14° 30' |
| M93 (NGC 2447) | 6th-magnitude open cluster |
| | RA 07h 44.6m Dec –23° 52' |

**Sagitta** – late summer

| M71 (NGC 6838) | 8th-magnitude globular cluster |
|---|---|
| | RA 19h 53.8m Dec +18° 47' |

**Sagittarius** – summer

| M8 (NGC 6523) | 6th-magnitude nebula |
|---|---|
| Lagoon Nebula | RA 18h 03.8m Dec –24° 23' |
| M17 (NGC 6618) | 6th-magnitude nebula |
| Omega Nebula | RA 18h 20.8m Dec –16° 11' |
| M18 (NGC 6613) | 7th-magnitude open cluster |
| | RA 18h 19.9m Dec –17 08' |
| M20 (NGC 6514) | 9th-magnitude nebula |
| Trifid Nebula | RA 18h 02.3m Dec –23° 02' |
| M21 (NGC 6531) | 6th-magnitude open cluster |
| | RA 18h 04.6m Dec –22° 30' |
| M22 (NGC 6656) | 5th-magnitude globular cluster |
| | RA 18h 36.4m Dec –23° 54' |
| M23 (NGC 6494) | 5th-magnitude open cluster |
| | RA 17h 56.8m Dec –19° 01' |
| M24 (NGC 6603) | 5th-magnitude open cluster |
| | RA 18h 16.9m Dec –18° 29' |
| M25 (IC 4725) | 5th-magnitude open cluster |
| | RA 18h 31.6m Dec –19° 15' |
| M28 (NGC 6626) | 7th-magnitude globular cluster |
| | RA 18h 24.5m Dec –24° 52' |
| M54 (NGC 6715) | 8th-magnitude globular cluster |
| | RA 18h 55.1m Dec –30° 29' |
| M55 (NGC 6809) | 7th-magnitude globular cluster |
| | RA 19h 40.0m Dec –30° 58' |
| M69 (NGC 6637) | 8th-magnitude globular cluster |
| | RA 18h 31.4m Dec –32° 21' |
| M70 (NGC 6681) | 8th-magnitude globular cluster |
| | RA 18h 43.2m Dec –32° 18' |
| M75 (NGC 6864) | 9th-magnitude globular cluster |
| | RA 20h 06.1m Dec –21° 55' |

**Scorpius (northern part)** – midsummer

| M4 (NGC 6121) | 6th-magnitude globular cluster |
|---|---|
| | RA 16h 23.6m Dec –26° 32' |
| M7 (NGC 6475) | 3rd-magnitude open cluster |
| | RA 17h 53.9m Dec –34° 49' |
| M80 (NGC 6093) | 7th-magnitude globular cluster |
| | RA 16h 17.0m Dec –22° 59' |

**Scutum** – mid to late summer

| M11 (NGC 6705) | 6th-magnitude open cluster |
|---|---|
| Wild Duck Cluster | RA 18h 51.1m Dec –06° 16' |

| M26 (NGC 6694) | 8th-magnitude open cluster |
|---|---|
| | RA 18h 45.2m Dec –09° 24' |

**Serpens** – summer

| M5 (NGC 5904) | 6th-magnitude globular cluster |
|---|---|
| | RA 15h 18.6m Dec +02° 05' |
| M16 (NGC 6611) | 6th-magnitude open cluster, |
| | surrounded by the Eagle Nebula. |
| | RA 18h 18.8m Dec –13° 47' |

**Taurus** – winter

| M1 (NGC 1952) | 8th-magnitude supernova remnant |
|---|---|
| Crab Nebula | RA 05h 34.5m Dec +22° 00' |
| M45 | 1st-magnitude open cluster, |
| Pleiades | an excellent binocular object. |
| | RA 03h 47.0m Dec +24° 07' |

**Triangulum** – autumn

| M33 (NGC 598) | 6th-magnitude spiral galaxy |
|---|---|
| | RA 01h 33.9m Dec +30° 39' |

**Ursa Major** – all year

| M81 (NGC 3031) | 7th-magnitude spiral galaxy |
|---|---|
| | RA 09h 55.6m Dec +69° 04' |
| M82 (NGC 3034) | 8th-magnitude starburst galaxy |
| | RA 09h 55.8m Dec +69° 41' |
| M97 (NGC 3587) | 12th-magnitude planetary nebula |
| Owl Nebula | RA 11h 14.8m Dec +55° 01' |
| M101 (NGC 5457) | 8th-magnitude spiral galaxy |
| | RA 14h 03.2m Dec +54° 21' |
| M108 (NGC 3556) | 10th-magnitude spiral galaxy |
| | RA 11h 11.5m Dec +55° 40' |
| M109 (NGC 3992) | 10th-magnitude spiral galaxy |
| | RA 11h 57.6m Dec +53° 23' |

**Virgo** – spring

| M49 (NGC 4472) | 8th-magnitude elliptical galaxy |
|---|---|
| | RA 12h 29.8m Dec +08° 00' |
| M58 (NGC 4579) | 10th-magnitude spiral galaxy |
| | RA 12h 37.7m Dec +11° 49' |
| M59 (NGC 4621) | 10th-magnitude elliptical galaxy |
| | RA 12h 42.0m Dec +11° 39' |
| M60 (NGC 4649) | 9th-magnitude elliptical galaxy |
| | RA 12h 43.7m Dec +11° 33' |
| M61 (NGC 4303) | 10th-magnitude spiral galaxy |
| | RA 12h 21.9m Dec +04° 28' |
| M84 (NGC 4374) | 9th-magnitude elliptical galaxy |
| | RA 12h 25.1m Dec +12° 53' |
| M86 (NGC 4406) | 9th-magnitude elliptical galaxy |
| | RA 12h 26.2m Dec +12° 57' |
| M87 (NGC 4486) | 9th-magnitude elliptical galaxy |
| | RA 12h 30.8m Dec +12° 24' |
| M89 (NGC 4552) | 10th-magnitude elliptical galaxy |
| | RA 12h 35.7m Dec +12° 33' |
| M90 (NGC 4569) | 9th-magnitude spiral galaxy |
| | RA 12h 36.8m Dec +13° 10' |
| M104 (NGC 4594) | Almost edge-on 8th-magnitude |
| Sombrero Galaxy | spiral galaxy. |
| | RA 12h 40.0m Dec –11° 37' |

**Vulpecula** – late summer and autumn

| M27 (NGC 6853) | 8th-magnitude planetary nebula |
|---|---|
| Dumbbell Nebula | RA 19h 59.6m Dec +22° 43' |

When choosing a telescope, it's always a good idea to set out your requirements first. How large a telescope can you cope with? What are your local conditions like? What are your observational interests? What's your budget? To this list, people often add that they would like to be able to take photos through their telescope. But this seemingly simple requirement can make a huge difference to your choice, and can easily end up being the dominant factor. So this article outlines the basics of what you need for astrophotography of different types, from the point of view of choosing the right kit.

Actually, astrophotography of all kinds has never been easier. Today, even suburban amateurs with fairly modest means can take pictures as good as or better than those which once came from the leading observatories. All this comes at a cost in cameras, equipment and time. So it's important to be aware before you start how long is the road which you have decided to take! And maybe there are ways of getting quite impressive results without going the whole hog.

### Photographing the Moon

The Moon is by far the easiest object to get started with. It's bright, easy to find in any telescope and often yields spectacular results. At its simplest, you can aim your scope at the Moon, point your camera into the eyepiece and take a snap. Quite often the result is impressive, and even mobile phone cameras can give stunning shots if you're lucky.

A more advanced approach is to use a single-lens reflex (SLR) camera, which allows you to remove its normal lens and attach it directly to the telescope in place of the eyepiece. The telescope then behaves exactly the same way as a long telephoto lens. You can get adapters for most modern digital SLR (DSLR) cameras, usually on the T-mount or T-ring system.

Once your camera is attached, you can snap away, ideally using a cable release so as not to jog the telescope when pressing the shutter button. In the case of the Moon, a typical exposure time will be a fraction of a second at ISO 100, during which time the Moon will not have drifted significantly through the field of view. So you don't need any kind of drive on the telescope.

### Photographing the planets

The set-up described above will work equally well with the bright planets. But most planetary photographers don't actually use weighty SLR cameras for their work. Instead, they use purpose-

▼ A DSLR camera attached directly to the telescope using an adapter. Notice that the camera focus point is fairly close to the telescope, and some focusers do not have enough travel to allow this.

made cameras based on webcam technology. Webcams are basically small video cameras which are used for chatting online. They provide a compressed video stream at much lower resolution than a full-sized camera, but they are lightweight and can give very good images.

Off-the-shelf webcams require a lot of modification before they can be attached to a telescope, but Celestron have their own purpose-built planetary camera, the NexImage, which is sold complete with an eyepiece adapter and software for linking it to the computer which is essential when undertaking this type of photography. Most people use a laptop computer for the purpose, usually near to the telescope. More advanced cameras are available which don't compress the individual images when producing the datastream, though at somewhat higher cost. The NexImage costs about £140 and more advanced models from The Imaging Source may cost two or three times that amount.

A webcam has a much smaller field of view than a DSLR camera, though the detail shown might be similar. But where the webcam scores is in its ability to record many frames per second in real time. As you watch the planet on the monitor, you can see that the image is usually both moving around slightly and becoming distorted as a result of the turbulence in our atmosphere – what astronomers call 'seeing'. With a webcam it's easy to record not just individual images but hundreds in a short time. Freely available software, such as Registax or AVIStack, then selects the best images and stacks them so as to reduce the electronic noise in the images. Image processing then sharpens the image, giving results of excellent quality even from small instruments.

Ideally, your telescope should have a motor drive for planetary photography, so as to keep the planet on the webcam's tiny chip for a few minutes at a time. But a precise drive isn't essential, as the software is designed to cope with some image movement.

### Photographing faint objects

Most deep-sky objects, and many Solar System objects such as comets, are much fainter than the Moon and planets, and require exposure times of the order of many seconds to minutes. Webcams are usually limited to brief exposures, but DSLR cameras can usually give exposures as long as you like. You can also get purpose-built

**SUPPLIERS OF THE EQUIPMENT MENTIONED HERE**

Sky-Watcher telescopes and autoguiders from Optical Vision: check www.opticalvision.co.uk for dealers

Meade telescopes and camera adapters from Telescope House: www.telescopehouse.com

Celestron NexImage: check www.celestron.uk.com for dealers

Autoguiding CCDs and accessories from Opticstar: www.opticstar.com

*Prices quoted here are current as of mid-2010.*

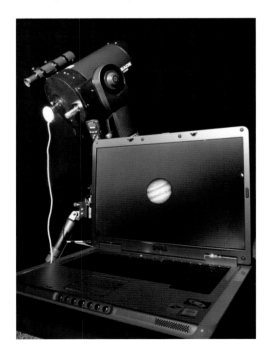

▼ A webcam is lightweight and can be attached to virtually any telescope. More advanced cameras give better images, and the best results come from mono cameras that require images to be taken through separate colour filters.

▲ *Peter Shah used this
200 mm reflecting telescope
to take the images on pages
8, 40 and 53. The CCD camera
is attached to the main scope,
while the smaller refracting
telescope has an autoguider
(not visible).*

CCD cameras with cooled chips to reduce electronic noise, and these are capable of giving really superb results, though they cost far more than a popular DSLR – in some cases thousands of pounds.

Apart from a camera, there are two prime requirements when taking long-exposure photos. One is an equatorial mount, which is aligned with the Earth's axis so as to counteract the daily turning of the heavens. A simple altazimuth mount, with up-down and left-right axes, as used on many instruments, is of little use for long exposures because the field of view will rotate along with the sky. The other requirement is an accurate motor drive. But the telescope drive that keeps Jupiter within the field of view for planetary imaging will probably be hopeless for exposure times longer than a few tens of seconds. Even a tiny error will be enough to turn a star image from a point into a streak.

Until recently, long exposures involved heroic efforts manually guiding on a star to overcome such errors. A few seconds' inattention at the end of a one-hour exposure could ruin the whole thing! But these days, autoguiding is the solution. This generally means having a separate telescope on the same mounting with a purpose-built autoguider attached, though there are ways in which you can use the same telescope. An autoguider consists of a separate CCD unit or even a webcam which takes an image of a star every second or so. Any drift of the star's image causes it to correct the drive rate to counteract it. Generally, you need a separate program running on your laptop to accomplish the autoguiding, but stand-alone autoguiders are now coming on to the market. These have a small display which shows the locations of stars in the field of view, from which you select one.

Autoguiders will work with a variety of the more advanced mounts which have separate autoguiding ports. These are often referred to as ST-4 ports, after the SBIG ST-4 unit which was the first widely used autoguider. Typical mounts include the Sky-Watcher Go To mounts such as the HEQ5, and the Celestron CG-5GT. Meade LX200 Schmidt-Cassegrain instruments are already on fork mounts which also have suitable autoguiding ports, and there are Meade accessories which will attach a separate telescope to the mounts. But if you are using an equatorial mount, you'll need to go to a third-party supplier for a suitable bar allowing you to put two telescopes on to the same mount. Many users also swear by the free PHD autoguiding software (www.stark-labs.com) which has clever autocalibration, rather than the software that comes with their autoguider.

▲ *Sky-Watcher's new Synguider, introduced in 2010, is stand-alone and needs no laptop. Once in focus, the screen at the back shows the positions of the stars in the field of view.*

But the whole business starts to get horribly complicated and indeed expensive. You need a suitable mount, your main telescope, a guide telescope, an autoguider, a camera to take the images and a laptop to control the whole thing, which together will probably cost at least £5,000. You have to polar-align your mount, connect up everything including power supplies for the mount, laptop and cameras, and then hope that it is still clear by the time you get round to taking the exposures! As one expert warned me, 'Don't forget the medical bills for stress as well!' But the upside is that, with perseverance, you can take superb images.

▲ *Telephoto lenses are ideal for wide-field shots, such as this 2005 view of the Pleiades star cluster and Comet Machholz, taken by Thierry Legault with a Canon 10D camera and 200 mm lens. The exposure time was 5 minutes at ISO 400.*

However, there is an easier way out, and that is to take images that are within the limitations of your equipment. The problems all stem from trying to take pictures at longer and longer focal lengths, which then require precision guiding. But if you use shorter focal lengths – say an ordinary 200 mm telephoto lens instead of your telescope – then you can get away with much less effort, and still take some striking photos. All you need to do is to piggyback your camera on top of the telescope. The drive will probably allow exposures of several minutes without any guiding. The field of view of a 200 mm lens on the average DLSR is just under $7 \times 5°$, which is about the same as many binoculars. Many star clusters, nebulae and even galaxies are well within its grasp, and such a combination is ideal if a good comet comes along. After all, the main thing is to get results which look good and might be worth framing for your wall!

▶ *Many telescope mounts include a threaded rod on the tube rings which allow you to attach a camera with a telephoto lens. Driven exposures of many minutes are often possible without autoguiding.*